INTERRUPTING
WHITE PRIVILEGE

INTERRUPTING WHITE PRIVILEGE

Catholic Theologians
Break the Silence

**Laurie M. Cassidy and Alex Mikulich,
Editors**

ORBIS BOOKS

Maryknoll, New York 10545

Founded in 1970, Orbis Books endeavors to publish works that enlighten the mind, nourish the spirit, and challenge the conscience. The publishing arm of the Maryknoll Fathers and Brothers, Orbis seeks to explore the global dimensions of the Christian faith and mission, to invite dialogue with diverse cultures and religious traditions, and to serve the cause of reconciliation and peace. The books published reflect the views of their authors and do not represent the official position of the Maryknoll Society. To learn more about Maryknoll and Orbis Books, please visit our website at www.maryknoll.org.

Published by Orbis Books, Maryknoll, New York 10545–0308.
Manufactured in the United States of America.
Manuscript editing and typesetting by Joan Weber Laflamme.

Library of Congress Cataloging-in-Publication Data

Interrupting white privilege : Catholic theologians break the silence / Laurie M. Cassidy and Alexander Mikulich, editors.
   p. cm.
 Includes bibliographical references.
 ISBN 978–1–57075–700–6 (pbk. : alk. paper)
 1. Racism—Religious aspects—Catholic Church. 2. Racism—Moral and ethical aspects. 3. Racism—Religious aspects—Christianity. 4. Racism—United States. 5. Race relations—Religious aspects—Catholic Church. 6. Race relations—Moral and ethical aspects. 7. Race relations—Religious aspects—Christianity. 8. Race relations—United States. I. Cassidy, Laurie M. II. Mikulich, Alexander.
 BX1795.R33I58 2007
 277.3'083089—dc22

                                                         2006033735

CONTENTS

v

ACKNOWLEDGMENTS

Spiritually, theologically, and practically, this book is indebted to a "cloud of witnesses." This project would never have begun or come to completion without many faithful and wise colleagues, co-workers, friends, and relatives. Although our names appear on the cover, there are many people, known and unknown, living and dead, upon whose backs we stand and in whose footsteps we humbly walk. We extend our deepest gratitude to mentors and colleagues who encouraged and enabled the White Privilege and Racism Developing Group of the Catholic Theological Society of America to begin in 2003 and who have continually provided theological wisdom, authentic witness to the gospel, inspiration, and practical assistance to the project: M. Shawn Copeland, Bryan N. Massingale, Margaret Eletta Guider, Jon Nilson, and Margaret Pfeil. We especially thank Barbara Hilkert Andolsen, who, since the inception of this project, became a generous mentor to the White Privilege and Racism Developing Group and without whom this book would never have become reality. We thank Mary E. Hobgood for her delightful hospitality and ongoing encouragement. We are especially grateful to all the contributors: their courage breaks silence and reveals new possibilities. And we are indebted to numerous colleagues who have contributed to the conversations of the White Privilege and Racism Developing Group, including Dawn Nothwehr, O.S.F., Christine Firer Hinze, Kevin Burke, S.J., John O'Brien, C.P., Michele Saracino, Colleen Carpenter Cullinan, and Cara Anthony. We thank past and present presidents of the Catholic Theological Society of America for making the White Privilege and Racism Developing Group a reality, including M. Shawn Copeland, Jon Nilson, Roberto Goizueta, Daniel Finn, and Catherine Hilkert.

We are deeply thankful to Susan Perry, editor at Orbis Books, whose graceful inspiration and practical support turned this project into a book.

I, Alex, thank my sister Mary Ann Nicholas, whose bone marrow gives me life, and Mark Hollingsworth, for inspiring me at a critical moment in this project. I thank Michael Schuck, William French, and John McCarthy, my mentors at Loyola University Chicago, whose wisdom opened me to new ways that religious social ethicists should address the U.S. legacy of white privilege and racism. I thank my colleagues at Saint Joseph College for invaluable support and mentoring: Billye Auclair, Clark Hendley, Ann Marie Caron, R.S.M., Joseph Cheah, O.S.M., Julius Rubin, and members of the Faculty Development Committee, who funded my annual trips to the meetings of the Catholic Theological Society of America.

I thank Pat Senich for helping me prepare the final manuscript. My contribution is indebted to the librarians of Saint Joseph College, especially Sheila Martin, Kathleen Kelley, Linda Geffner, Lynne Piacentini, Ann Williams, and Antoinette Collins. I am grateful to students at Saint Joseph College, who daily teach me how to address white male privilege. I thank friends from West Hartford Conversations on Race, especially Wanda Correa, who challenge me in the struggle for racial justice. I thank brothers and sisters from the Office of Black Catholic Ministries and of Saint Michael Parish in Hartford, who are true witnesses to the love of the gospel. Kind and critical comments from Deacon Arthur Miller and historian Jeffrey O. G. Ogbar helped refine the prospectus.

My deepest thanks and love goes to my wife, Kara, whose love nurtures joy daily and whose practical wisdom helps shape my work with beauty. I dedicate my contribution to her and our children, that they may experience new possibilities for a world free of racial oppression.

I, Laurie, am grateful to various communities of people inside and outside the academy. I am indebted to Carol Brennan and the young people who in the 1980s invited me to work with them at St. Paul's Parish in Dorchester, Massachusetts. Their experiences, insight, and challenges opened my eyes to hear the gospel in a whole new way. I am grateful to colleagues in the A. K. Rice Institute, especially Betsy Hasegawa, Linda C. Powell, and Terri

Monroe, R.S.C.J., for their probing questions that enabled me to grapple with my own white identity formation.

I am thankful to the folks at the Women's Theological Center. Working with Donna Bivens, Meck Groot, Sonja Latimore, Jacqui Lindsay, Nancy Richardson, and other board members of the center was an inspiring and sustaining experience. Colleagues and students at Trinity College in Hartford, Connecticut, offered me enormous encouragement. Ellison Banks Findly, Leslie Desmangles, and Patricia Byrne, C.S.J., encouraged me at every turn with this project and pushed me to see its connection to teaching. Liz Moore, Trevor Hyde, Ryan Harrity, Mark Durney, Kristen Chin, Joe Kenol, and Chris Moore are among the students who both within and outside the classroom have helped me think through what it means to live in the matrix of domination.

I have been blessed to have an ongoing conversation about race with my friend Anmol Satiani, who introduced me to the community of scholars and activists involved with Janet Helm's annual "Diversity Challenge" conference at Boston College. Finally, two women have blessed me with their kindness and inspired me in their scholarship: Jamie T. Phelps, O.P., enabled me to understand that what I had learned at a grassroots level could and must be translated into academic discourse, and the generous encouragement and wisdom of M. Shawn Copeland continues to inform that translation.

INTRODUCTION

Laurie M. Cassidy and Alex Mikulich

> What I'm hearing, which is sort of scary, is they all want to stay in Texas. Everyone is so overwhelmed by the hospitality. And so many people in the arena here, you know, were underprivileged anyway, so this is working out well for them.[1]

This profoundly disturbing comment by Barbara Bush about displaced families after Hurricane Katrina exposes unquestioned assumptions of white privilege. These displaced human beings call us to rip back the veil covering the dynamics of white privilege that legitimate their suffering. This book uses the tools we have inherited as Catholic theologians and ethicists to confront the racism and white privilege that make such a comment possible.

Though many white Americans may have found Mrs. Bush's comments insensitive or offensive, what she reveals about white privilege may be a hard truth to swallow for those same Americans. As Barbara Andolsen points out in this volume, 71 percent of blacks said the response to Katrina demonstrated racial inequality, while 56 percent of whites did not agree with that statement. However, the picture on the ground substantiates a shameful truth. A year after Katrina, Kavita Ramdas of the Global Fund for Women recalls, "You saw these poor women on TV in . . . unspeakable circumstances. It could have been Haiti, but it was America."[2] Katrina survivors continue to live in "third-world" circumstances, and poor women of color have it the worst.[3]

The intersection of race, class, and gender oppression at work in the response to Hurricane Katrina has been difficult for many white people to acknowledge. Hurricane Katrina demonstrated that racism is not something in the past, but a disease inside human hearts and minds and reified in the structures that condition everyday life. In the words of Iris Marion Young, "Trying to identify the cabal of bigots whose intended goal is to keep blacks down is easier than coming to terms with the paradox that normal practices within which people act with good intentions continue to produce significant evil."[4] Hurricane Katrina exposed the reality that our "normal" way of life creates an evil that makes its home here—within us—not in some distant land.

Hurricane Katrina was not an isolated incident of race, class, and gender oppression in the United States. Because of our troubling contemporary context and history as Americans, our volume calls Roman Catholic theologians and ethicists to engage critically and constructively the theological and ethical imperative of the ongoing legacy of white privilege and racism. Our work does not set out to prove to the reader that racism and white privilege exist but seeks rather to describe these realities and to invite a collective response from the white U.S. Catholic community. Whether a bishop, administrator, educator, pastor, deacon, lay leader, or parishioner, and especially our Catholic colleagues in ethics and theology, each has a gift and responsibility to manifest the Spirit for the common good (1 Cor 12:7) in the face of the evil of white privilege.

Though there is a variety of understandings of racism in this volume, we invite the reader to consider racism as "*a system by which one race maintains supremacy over another race through a set of attitudes, behaviors, social structures, ideologies, and the requisite power needed to impose them.*"[5] Racism is not something "out there," unrelated to our white existence.[6] Without understanding and acknowledging white privilege, "racism can, in short, be conceived as something external . . . rather than as a system that shapes [the white person's] daily existence and sense of self."[7]

In these essays we explore as white theologians and ethicists how our privilege creates the conditions of racism in the United States and around the world. The term *white privilege* attempts to make intelligible all the benefits that come simply from the fact that one is born with white skin. We suggest Peggy McIntosh's working definition of white privilege as "unearned advantage and conferred dominance."[8]

Moreover, racism and white privilege are two dimensions of the complex reality of dominance and subordination that infect everyday relations. Patricia Hill Collins characterizes all relationships as being interconnected within a web—a matrix of domination—within which all of us participate in every moment of our "normal" living. Collins explains this web as a matrix of domination that involves interlocking systems of oppression. To understand white privilege through the lens of the matrix of domination opens up deeper understandings of the varying degrees of penalty and privilege that pervade relationships in everyday existence. Seeing race, class, and gender as well as heterosexism, anti-Semitism, and imperialism as interlocking but not interchangeable opens up possibilities of a both/and rather than an either/or stance "in which all groups possess varying amounts of penalty and privilege in one historically created system."[9] Collins explains: "In this system, for example, white women are penalized by their gender but privileged by their race. Depending on the context, an individual may be an oppressor, a member of an oppressed group, or simultaneously oppressor and oppressed."[10] Collins adds that understanding oppression through interlocking systems enables the recognition that the matrix of domination contains few pure victims or oppressors. In other words, "each individual derives varying amounts of penalty and privilege from the multiple systems of oppression which frame everyone's life."[11]

By interrogating racism and white privilege from within this context of the matrix of domination, our volume pushes forward a self-critical and nuanced ability by white Catholics to analyze and address the varieties of privilege and penalty that are operative in specific social locations within which we live and work. This work is an imperative of our baptism into the body of Christ, the gift and task of manifesting the Spirit for the common good.

Turn back to the cover of this book. What do you see? Is anyone present at this crossroads where two paths intersect in a quiet park? Why isn't anyone sitting on the bench to enjoy the peace and quiet? Perhaps we white theologians simply assume that everything is peaceful. However, too often those of us who are white are not cognizant of the history that conditions our everyday existence. For example, might this have been a site of lynching? Or was this a place of victory for the Lakota fighting Custer? The crossroads of history is a place of victimization and victory. White people do not know the human stories at this crossroads, or we have recast history for our own benefit.

In Chapter 6, Margaret Eletta Guider invites readers to remember how this anthology stands on the shoulders of white Catholic pioneers such as John LaFarge, Yves Congar, Austin Flannery, Thomas Merton, Rosemary Radford Ruether, Anne Patrick, Walter Buhlman, Daniel Berrigan, Johannes B. Metz, Albert Nolan, and Richard McBrien. However, we are implicated by the general silence in our profession in regard to racism and white privilege. The silence of white theologians bespeaks the contradiction between our claims for a universal, ontological human equality and the reality of the social, political, and economic privilege white theologians and ethicists consciously and unconsciously accept and assume. Piecemeal efforts to address the structural and institutional sin of white privilege and racism repeatedly prove insufficient. The late Joseph Nearon's clarion call to Catholic theologians largely remains unheeded:

> Catholic theology is racist. If this fact can be blamed on the cultural situation, if it is more the result of omission and inattention than conscious commission it is still a fact. There is an insensitivity here which can only remain blameless until it has been pointed out and I serve notice to you, my colleagues, and I am now pointing it out. . . . I do this not to condemn, but to awaken.[12]

As Roman Catholic theologians we intend that this book will signal that silence or neutrality in the face of this evil is no longer acceptable in the theological academy, church, or society.[13] We propose a novel Roman Catholic collective and dialogical conversation among theology, spirituality, and social ethics to explicate the theological significance of white privilege and racism. *Interrupting White Privilege* continues a process of redressing a silence that black Catholic theologian Jamie Phelps compares to that of leading German theologians in the face of the Nazis' "final solution" against the Jewish people.[14] While some may find

Phelps's comparison unwarranted or harsh, Jon Nilson details evidence in support of her claim in Chapter 1.

Roman Catholic theology and social teaching unify the essays collected in this volume. Central to Catholic moral thought is the question of "the good": how it is imagined, understood, and lived out in particular historical circumstances. *Interrupting White Privilege* unveils two working assumptions about this central Catholic theological and moral category: (1) theologians' understanding of the good is always conditioned by the cultural, social, and historical situation in which they find themselves;[15] and (2) imagining, defining, and realizing the good has been deeply conditioned by the "colorblindness" and racism of North American theology and ethics.[16]

Evidence of this lacuna can be seen in the U.S. bishops' letter *Brothers and Sisters to Us*, which lacks the analysis and depth seen in similar statements on the economy and on peace.[17] In addition, statements by the U.S. bishops on race have received little scholarly attention.[18] An orienting question emerges from these assumptions for North American Catholic theologians. How do we conceive of and speak of the good in a country with a history of slavery and ongoing racism, and within a community of discourse "which is marred by racial prejudice, malice, ignorance, indifference and deception?"[19]

Exploring this question and its impact on Roman Catholic theology and ethics in the United States will involve understanding racism not only as a moral evil that is inflicted upon people of color, but as a social sin maintained through systems of white privilege. This entails bringing to bear sophisticated forms of interdisciplinary analysis that will render theological, spiritual, and social ethical critiques of whiteness in the United States. Speaking of the good further demands that we utilize the rich resources of ethicists and theologians of color from the United States. Learning from these resources, we hope, will shift white people's perspective of people of color from being objects of white study to our recognition of them as subjects who are "capable of independent action or creative initiative which can shape white response."[20]

The inspiration for this volume originated within the Roman Catholic theological academy in response to multiple calls from our colleagues of color. One of the primary inspirations for this volume is M. Shawn Copeland's guest editorial in the December 2000 issue of *Theological Studies* devoted to the "Catholic Reception of Black Theology." Copeland wrote:

> When will White Catholic theologians acknowledge the insights of Black theology as permanently valid theological achievements? . . . White racist supremacy is the scotoma of Catholic theology. If there is need for a serious and exacting Black Catholic theology that goes well beyond historical retrieval, then there is an even more urgent need for White Catholic theologians to critique White racist supremacy within Church and society.[21]

Copeland's indictment inspired a collaborative initiative by Margaret Pfeil, Laurie Cassidy, and Alex Mikulich to develop an ongoing session to address white privilege and racism within the Catholic Theological Society of America (CTSA). We designed the initial session to provide an opportunity for critical reflection upon the tasks of analyzing and dismantling white privilege as constitutive activities of the vocation of the white Roman Catholic theologian. The initial questions in our discussion involved how to develop this commitment in the classroom and among faculties in many theologians' home institutions. Participants offered specific resources for course and curriculum development to educate students on the realities of racism and white privilege and strategies for advancing racial justice. In addition, we explored examples of institutional processes to "de-center" the normative assumptions of whiteness among faculties. Our own teaching and these conversations guide the organization and goals of this book. We provide a resource section for teaching and learning that includes questions for each chapter, a select bibliography, Web resources, and a selection of Catholic dioceses and organizations committed to long term anti-racist vision plans.

Initial work by past presidents Richard McBrien and Anne Patrick highlighted the problem of racism in the CTSA and paved the way for recent developments.[22] Unlike these previous initiatives on the reality of racism, Margaret Guider addressed racism not only as a radical evil inflicted upon the lives of people of color, but also as a moral problem that involves white people coming to terms with privilege. The work of Margaret Guider and Jon Nilson signifies a profound change in perspective on racism within the CTSA. Guider and Nilson are *white* theologians demonstrating to *white* theologians the racism of our profession, and that this is a moral dilemma for *white* theologians.[23] These declarations are not new; however, those making the declarations are. The statement of these white theologians signifies a *kairos* moment—at this crucial crossroads of history—for Roman Catholic theologians to redress their silence on arguably one of the most serious human rights violations in American history.[24]

The image of crossroads implies that history is a place of intersection, a place of human connection and disconnection, liberation and oppression. The crossroads is a site of multiple forms of oppression, as well as histories of struggle and claims of agency. As white theologians it is our responsibility to call attention to the silence *and* to the possibilities created at the crossroads where we live. *Interrupting White Privilege* seeks to do just this.

This volume promotes theological research and engagement in relationship to the moral imperative of addressing white privilege and provides one way for Roman Catholic theologians, ethicists, clergy, lay leaders, adult people of faith, and upper-level college and graduate students to engage theological, spiritual, moral, and social scientific resources addressing white racial privilege.

Part I sets the historical context of theological engagement with race and racism since Vatican II. Jon Nilson confesses his own racism through an analysis of the ways Roman Catholic theologians failed to respond to black theology and to address white privilege. Mary Elizabeth Hobgood extends her original work on the relationship between sexual and economic ethics that she began in her ground-breaking *Dismantling Privilege: An Ethics of Accountability*. In Chapter 2 she demonstrates how whites are damaged humanly, morally, spiritually, and economically by racism. Hobgood argues that structures supporting white privilege and racism will not change until the shame, fear, dissociation, and projected hatred of white embodiment are mitigated by a self-acceptance of the vulnerability and vitality of being human. Barbara Hilkert Andolsen contributes the third chapter of Part I, arguing that theologians and ethicists need the social sciences. Utilizing interdisciplinary tools to examine practical and moral responses to citizens in the wake of Hurricane Katrina, Andolsen asks how U.S. Catholic theologians will draw upon social-scientific research to develop understanding of the social sin of racism and the conversion to which we are called. Part I thus sets the stakes of this volume in historical, spiritual, moral, economic, and social-scientific terms.

Part II shifts attention to the ways three senior theologians name white privilege and racism. In Chapter 4, Charles Curran explains the process of coming to consciousness of his social location and his recognition of the impact of this privilege on his work. Curran argues that because white privilege is an invisible and systemic reality, the only way to confront it is through personal, intellectual, and spiritual conversion. Roger Haight proposes the idea of dismantling white privilege as a dysfunctional rhetoric in Chapter 5. Haight draws upon the notion of "negative contrast experience"—those situations of injustice, oppression, and suffering in which human beings cry out, "This should not be!" Haight argues that in this framework white privilege is not a dialectically positive concept relative to racism but precisely a further analysis of racism itself. As a positive notion in dialectical tension with racism, a concept of "racial solidarity" corresponds with basic Christian premises and ideals, and with common values both in American society and an increasingly globalized world. The concept of "racial solidarity" evokes the utopic dream of Martin Luther King Jr. that also engaged whites. Part II concludes with Margaret Guider's analysis of racism in relation to the mission of the church. She argues, through the lens of Vatican II's *Missio ad Gentes*, that white privilege and racism are the most serious forms of counter-witness to the gospel, and she suggests an alternative vision and practice.

Part III includes three constructive theological engagements with white privilege and racism. As a constitutive dimension of discipleship, Margaret Pfeil argues that the option for the poor provides an epistemology that issues in a course of action for every Christian vocation, including that of the theologian. Dismantling white privilege requires that white Americans put themselves in jeopardy, resisting institutionalized racism by challenging white supremacist practices and assumptions in the structuring of determinative indices of the common good like education, housing, and hiring policies. Solidarity means inviting other whites to adopt a conception of social power as generative rather than divisive. By noticing the intersections of race, class, and gender as they affect the most vulnerable in society, all may work toward securing not the relative advantage of any one group over another but rather the common good of the whole community.

Laurie Cassidy pursues similar reasoning, arguing that whites might constructively engage the black image of God developed by James Cone. Drawing upon the racial-contract theory of Charles Mills, Cassidy demonstrates the epistemological blindness inherent in whiteness that disables white theologians in critically assessing and dismantling white privilege. Utilizing James Cone's notion of "becoming Black with God," she suggests a spirituality that creates the possibility of white theologians overcoming the blindness of privilege and confronting racism. Cassidy argues that Cone's metaphor "God is Black" holds a radically disclosive power. Cone's juxtaposition of "God" with "Black" is a theological lens allowing white theologians to see "whiteness" in stark contrast to the God of Jesus. The attendant ethical demand to "become Black with God" signifies a profound spiritual journey in which epistemological blindness is healed through God's drawing the white theologian into solidarity with the oppressed.

Alex Mikulich's constructive engagement of white male privilege concludes Part III. Mikulich reinterprets Nicholas of Cusa's "learned ignorance" through M. Shawn Copeland's praxis of solidarity as a way to address white male privilege. He suggests that a praxis of solidarity before the cross may create the condition of the possibility of white male theologians taking responsibility for their complicity in racial privilege and seeking communal repentance for such sinfulness. A way of learning white male ignorance entails looking into the mirror of "Blackness" and seeing ourselves the way our brothers and sisters of color have seen us for over five hundred years. Lived conversion through solidarity and learned ignorance form the crossroads to which we are called, the place where our hearts may be re-tuned by Jesus, the place where we may yet find the grace to work through the contradictions of white male privilege.

Interrupting White Privilege is distinct from yet complements existing books addressing white privilege and racism. *Disrupting*

White Supremacy from Within: White People on What We Need to Do by Jennifer Harvey, Karin A. Case, and Robin Hawley Gorsline provides an excellent critical analysis of white racial privilege from Protestant perspectives. *Interrupting White Privilege* offers in-depth reflections from Roman Catholic theologians who incorporate a variety of multidisciplinary approaches. James W. Perkinson's *White Theology: Outing Supremacy in Modernity* and *Shamanism, Racism, and Hip Hop Culture* present one Protestant theologian's critique of white male privilege in modernity and his original interpretation of African religious traditions, racism, and hip-hop culture for theological praxis and pedagogy.

Our book contributes a novel collective, dialogical method of intra-racial and cross-racial conversation and praxis that explicates the theological significance of dismantling white racial privilege in the academy, church, and society. This book is a beginning, not an end. The essays here, we hope, break the silence of Catholic white privilege and draw all of us into a shared struggle of creative intra-racial and cross-racial spiritual, theological, and moral work that has yet to be done.

Notes

[1] Barbara Bush made this comment during a radio interview for the program "Marketplace" on American Public Media. "Mrs. Bush's remarks were 'observation,'" *The Boston Globe* (September 8, 2005), at http://www.boston.com (accessed August 8, 2006).

[2] "One Year Later, There's Still No Help for Katrina Victims," *Glamour* (August 2006): 170.

[3] Ibid.

[4] Iris Marion Young, "Katrina: Too Much Blame, Not Enough Responsibility," *Dissent* 53 (Winter 2006): 42.

[5] Margaret Eletta Guider, O.S.F., "Moral Imagination and *Missio ad Gentes*: Redressing the Counterwitness of Racism," *Proceedings of the Catholic Theological Society of America* 56 (2001): 54.

[6] We hold neither colorblindness nor an essentialist understanding of race. The basic notion of race in this volume is rooted in critical race theory: "Race and races are a product of social thought and relations. Not objective, inherent, or fixed, they correspond to no

biological or genetic reality; rather, races are categories that society invents, manipulates, or retires when convenient." See Richard Delgado and Jean Stefancic, *Critical Race Theory: An Introduction* (New York: NYU Press, 2001), 7.

[7] Ruth Frankenberg, *White Women, Race Matters: The Social Construction of Whiteness* (Minneapolis: University of Minnesota Press, 1993), 6.

[8] Peggy McIntosh, "White Privilege: Unpacking the Invisible Knapsack," *Peace and Freedom* (July/August 1989): 11–12.

[9] Patricia Hill Collins, *Fighting Words: Black Women and the Search for Justice* (Minneapolis: University of Minnesota Press, 1998), 225.

[10] Ibid.

[11] Ibid., 229.

[12] Joseph Nearon, "Preliminary Report. Research Committee for Black Theology," *Proceedings of the Catholic Theological Society of America* 29 (1974): 415.

[13] "White theologians who do not oppose racism publicly and rigorously engage it in their writings are part of the problem and must be exposed as the enemies of justice." See James Cone, "Looking Back, Going Forward: Black Theology as Public Theology," in *Black Faith and Public Talk*, ed. Dwight N. Hopkins (Maryknoll, NY: Orbis Books, 1999), 257.

[14] Jamie T. Phelps, O.P., "Communion Ecclesiology and Black Liberation Theology," *Theological Studies* 61, no. 4 (2000): 692.

[15] Bryan Massingale, "The African American Experience and U.S. Roman Catholic Ethics: 'Strangers and Aliens No Longer?'" in *Black and Catholic: The Challenge and Gift of Black Folk*, ed. Jamie T. Phelps (Milwaukee: Marquette University Press, 1997), 79.

[16] Theodore Walker, *Empower the People: Social Ethics for the African-American Church* (Maryknoll, NY: Orbis Books, 1991), 3.

[17] Massingale, "The African American Experience and U.S. Roman Catholic Ethics," 86.

[18] Ibid., 98.

[19] Ibid., 80.

[20] Ibid., 84.

[21] M. Shawn Copeland, "Guest Editorial," *Theological Studies* 61, no. 4 (2000): 605.

[22] Nearon, "Preliminary Report: Research Committee for Black Theology," 415.

[23] Guider, "Moral Imagination and *Missio ad Gentes*," 49–69; Jon Nilson, "Presidential Address: Confessions of a White Catholic Racist Theologian," *Proceedings of the Catholic Theological Society of America* 58 (2003): 64–82.

[24] Bryan Massingale, "African American Experience and U.S. Roman Catholic Ethics," 86.

PART I

CLAIMING DANGEROUS MEMORIES

White Privilege in Historical Context

1

• • • •

CONFESSIONS OF A WHITE CATHOLIC RACIST THEOLOGIAN

Jon Nilson

In this essay, I am trying to respond to three challenges. The first one comes from M. Shawn Copeland, who asks:

> How are we theologians to speak God's word in these times? How are we to understand our theological vocation? How are we to offer what we have to the struggle for authentic human liberation from within our culture? How shall the next generation of theologians remember us and the age in which we have come of age? Shall we be shamed into confessing that our shoulders sagged in recognition of the cost of truth? Shall we surrender our most cherished principles and values to expediency? Shall we be forced to admit that the cost of our own religious, moral, and intellectual conversion was too steep? What do our times call on theologians to become?[1]

The second challenge is a question from James H. Cone. Its barb is even sharper. Cone writes, "Racism is one of the great contradictions of the gospel in modern times. White theologians

This is a revision of an article titled "Confessions of a White Racist Catholic Theologian," published in *Proceedings of the Catholic Theological Society of America* 58 (2003): 64–82.

15

who do not oppose racism publicly and rigorously engage it in their writings are part of the problem and must be exposed as the enemies of justice. No one, therefore, can be neutral or silent in the face of this great evil."[2]

We Catholic theologians are among these silent white theologians, and Cone summons us in particular to account for ourselves. "What is it," he asks, "that renders White Catholic . . . theologians silent in regard to racism, even though they have been very outspoken about anti-Semitism and class and gender contradictions in response to radical protest?"[3] For Cone, a real theologian cannot choose whether or not to confront racism. "Racism is a profound contradiction of the gospel. . . . [Therefore] . . . any theology that does not fight White supremacy with all its intellectual strength cancels its Christian identity."[4] How, then, do so many of us manage to see so clearly that classism and sexism destroy the credibility of any Christian theology, yet fail to see that racism does the same?

The third challenge comes from Jamie Phelps and appears in *Theological Studies* (December 2000). This issue was devoted to the theme "The Catholic Reception of Black Theology." The authors of its articles are well known to the U.S. Catholic theological community. Their analyses show that this special issue would have been more accurately titled "The Catholic Marginalization of Black Theology." This point is made most sharply by Phelps when she describes white Catholic theological silence thus: "The silence of U.S. Catholic theologians about racism is parallel to the silence of leading German theologians and intellectuals during the Nazi atrocities and prosecution of the so-called 'final solution' against the Jewish people."[5] If ever there were a sentence that seems to come right off the page and seize the white reader by the throat, it is this one. It demands a response.

An initial reaction might well be to dismiss Phelps's claim as rhetorical overkill, simply a tactic to get whites to pay more attention to issues that she thinks are important. But that reaction is born of ignorance. Her comparison of white Catholic theologians to the German theologians is more than justified by Basil Davidson's conclusion that the slave trade "cost Africa at least fifty million souls";[6] by the extremes of suffering endured by the kidnapped Africans and their descendants for 244 years of legalized slavery;[7] by the 71 years of oppression and discrimination known as Jim Crow; by the 51 of those same years during which one black person was lynched about every two and a half days somewhere in the United States "at the hands of persons unknown";[8] and it is more than justified because racism continues to infect our country today.

The German theologians under National Socialism are an easy target for criticism and condemnation. They provide illusory reassurances of our moral superiority. But Phelps's analogy says to the Catholic theological community, "If you want to see someone who has failed to meet the responsibility of being a Catholic theologian when it comes to one of the greatest, if not the greatest, moral issue of our nation, just look in your mirror." For decades Johann Baptist Metz has borne the burden of being a German Catholic theologian in the "Christian" nation that gave birth to Nazism,[9] but there is no one like Metz here. No U.S. white Catholic theologian has taken on the burden of racism. Very few white Catholic theologians (except for Richard P. McBrien, Rosemary Radford Ruether, William O'Neill, Lisa Sowle Cahill, Daniel McGuire, and David Tracy) seem to have noticed much less published responses to black theology.

So Cone's question returns more forcefully. Why don't we have any theologians like Metz? Is it possible that, by and large, U.S. white Catholic theologians are racists? Surely not, if racism means night riders, lynchings, cross burnings, and race riots. Atrocities like these are light years away from the sedate world of theological libraries and seminar rooms. Surely not, if racism means simply the attitudes, words, and actions of individuals who discriminate openly and consciously against others on the basis of their skin color.

But what if racism is more pervasive and subtle? What if racism is more a system than a symptom? James Boggs's understanding of racism is more perceptive:

> The first thing we have to understand is that racism is not a "mental quirk" or a "psychological flaw" on an individual's part. Racism is the systematized oppression of one race by another. In other words, the various forms of oppression within every sphere of social relations—economic exploitation, military subjugation, political subordination, cultural devaluation, psychological violation, sexual degradation,

verbal abuse, etc.—together make up a whole of interact-
ing and developing processes which operate so normally
and naturally and are so much a part of the existing institutions of the society that the individuals involved are barely
conscious of their operation. As Fanon says, "The racist in
a culture with racism is therefore normal."[10]

Thus, racism makes oppression seem normal, preferred, legitimate, and, therefore, hard to detect and uproot precisely because
it is part of "the way things are" and "the way things ought to
be."

Now there is a type of racism peculiar to white Catholic theologians. It consists of ignoring, marginalizing, and dismissing that
body of theological insight and challenge born of the black struggle
for justice, black theology.[11]

So I have to confess that I am a racist. I am a racist insofar as
I rarely read and never cited any black theologians in my own
publications. I never suspected that the black churches might teach
me something that would make me a better Roman Catholic
ecclesiologist. Occasionally, I have assigned a short article by a
black theologian to my students but never a complete book. I
have learned much from other forms of Latin American and feminist liberation theology but paid little attention to black theology. So Cone is talking about me when he writes: "They engage
Feminist, Latin American, and other White reflections on God.
Why are they silent on Black theological reflections? If one read
only White Catholic theologians, one would hardly know that
Blacks exist in America or had the capacity for thought about
God."[12] Along with James Cone, Bryan Massingale has convinced
me that I am certainly not the only white Catholic racist theologian working today.[13]

It did not have to be this way. White Catholic theologians
could have been dialogue partners with black theology from the
very beginning. Thirty years ago, just four years after James Cone
published his ground-breaking *Black Theology and Black Power*,
Preston Williams addressed the Catholic Theological Society of
America and urged its membership to find, mentor, and support
the black Catholic scholars who were so urgently needed.[14] Then,
one year later, in 1974, Joseph Nearon delivered the preliminary

report of the Research Committee for Black Theology to the CTSA. At this point Nearon was a committee of one. "When President [Richard P.] McBrien asked me to take on this task," he said, "we decided that for the CTSA to address the question of black theology we needed someone who was (1) black, (2) Catholic, (3) a theologian. I noted that 'the field is fairly limited' and McBrien immediately responded 'To my knowledge you *are* the field.'"[15]

McBrien's invitation was the occasion for Nearon's own awakening, because black theology was uncharted territory for him, too. Although he was black, his blackness had played no role in his religious life or theological career up to that point. So, before he could chair this research committee, he felt the need to educate himself. Yet, even at this early stage of his work, Nearon could say to the CTSA:

> Catholic theology is racist. If this fact can be blamed on the cultural situation, if it is more the result of omission and inattention than conscious commission it is still a fact. There is an insensitivity here which can only remain blameless until it has been pointed out and I serve notice to you, my colleagues, that I am now pointing it out. . . . I do this not to condemn, but to awaken.[16]

If Catholic theology in this country was racist in the early 1970s, you might suppose that the theologians would have acknowledged Nearon's critique and would have done what needed to be done to overcome it. Still, however, the theological journals, publishers' catalogs (excepting Orbis Books, of course), graduate course curricula, and undergraduate course syllabi that make up theologians' stock in trade show little evidence that black theology even exists. How can we deny Cone's caustic observation: "If one read only White Catholic theologians, one would hardly know that Blacks exist in America or had the capacity for thought about God."[17]

Now this white Catholic marginalization of black theology makes a statement to black Christians. It says, "Your experience of struggle, suffering, and triumph and your Christian reflections on your experience *do not count*." This is the cultural devaluation and psychological violation that constitute racism. Whites are its victims, too. To declare, in effect, that the slave trade's cost of fifty million ancestors, that the torture endured by the slaves and their descendants, that the martyrdom of Christian slaves at the hands of slaveholders outraged by their slaves' conviction that God loved them and wanted their freedom,[18] that the degradation of Jim Crow and the reign of terror known as lynching, that the faith-born and faith-nurtured resistance to these atrocities, which was sung in the black spirituals, proclaimed in black preaching, interrogated in black theology—to declare implicitly that all this has nothing significant to contribute to a Catholic Christian understanding of the gospel for our time and nation is a drastic truncation and impoverishment of Catholic theology.

Once a church of feared and despised immigrants, American Catholicism is now the largest denomination in the United States. Its traditions, convictions, and values are preserved and pondered in over two hundred colleges and universities across the country. Seen through black eyes, however, the theological faculties of these institutions labor under a massive disability, namely, the illusion that black people who have lived the gospel throughout centuries of intense suffering have nothing significant to teach us about a tortured and crucified Lord. The question is, how could this marginalization of racism as a theological issue and of black theology as worthy of Catholic theological engagement come to be normal, legitimate, accepted, and utterly unremarkable? How could we Roman Catholic theologians have done this with untroubled consciences?

White Catholic Theological Racism: Why?

Four factors have been chiefly responsible: the realities of segregation, the ideal of integration, the impact of Vatican II in the United States, and the style of early black theology itself.

The Realities of Segregation

Between 1820 and 1920 well over thirty-three million European Catholics immigrated to the United States.[19] Most of these settled in the cities on the Eastern seaboard and the Midwest.[20]

At mid twentieth century, 1950, 75 percent of the nation's Catholics still lived in the Northeast and the Midwest.[21] The bishops were understandably driven by the priorities of maintenance, not mission, since they had to make provision for these millions. Their problem was how to serve these Catholics, how to tend the flocks they had, not to seek new sheep. They also had to maintain the unity of the church amid the tensions and conflicts between and within the various Catholic ethnic groups. The solution to the problem entailed a particular configuration of parish, neighborhood, and ethnicity.

By the end of the 1950s most urban whites in the North were Catholic. Thus, black-white relations in the urban North became black-Catholic relations,[22] since these same cities were also the destinations of black Americans seeking a better life for themselves and their families. "Between 1910 and 1940, 1,750,000 black people left the South. As a result, the black population outside the South doubled by 1940." The decade between 1910 and 1920 was the high point of the "Great Migration" from the rural South. In just these ten years the black populations of fifteen Northern cities grew by 50 percent or more; in some cases, the increase was dramatic, such as Chicago's 148 percent, Cleveland's 307 percent, Detroit's 611 percent, Akron's 749 percent, and Gary's nearly 1300 percent.[23]

As McGreevy's history, *Parish Boundaries*, shows, the influx of blacks was perceived as a mortal threat to nearly everything that Catholics held dear. "For generations," he points out, "Catholics . . . throughout the country . . . had absorbed a gospel linking neighborhood, family, and parish."[24] The prospect of integration meant "the possible loss of a home [the family's chief financial asset], the transformation of a familiar neighborhood into a ghetto—a threat to family, community and, not least of all, to the Church itself."[25] The prospect of integration, followed, as it nearly always was, by white Catholic flight from the area, meant the loss of all the church's facilities—the church building, the school, and, yes, the gymnasium—that their parents and grandparents had sacrificed so much to erect and maintain. Bishops and priests realized that they would lose not only these infrastructures but also the loyalty of the people in the pews if they pushed integration too hard from their pulpits.[26] "Integration" did not mean "equality of all God's children and Christ's redeemed" to these people, but instead, cultural, financial, and religious disaster.

It is bad enough that residential segregation was—and is—the main obstacle to black social advancement because it severely restricts "access to quality education, health care, employment and informal networking."[27] Urban residential segregation also guaranteed that few Catholics and few Catholic theologians would have anything close to friendship with a black person. Without such friendships, there was nothing to impel white Catholics to explore how racial differences could transform an "other" into a "beloved other" and what gifts these differences might bring to the church.

Throughout the formative years of most of us Catholic theologians, we saw no faces that made black suffering as intolerable to us as to the victims. We heard no voices that made black claims uncomfortable and inescapable for us. John Howard Griffin's small classic, *Black Like Me*, was a valiant effort to awaken whites to the reality of black suffering, but Griffin the white man traveled as a black man through the South, not the North. Therefore, most Catholics, even if they had read *Black Like Me*, could say, "It's not our problem here." Yet Martin Luther King Jr. maintained, "I have never seen—even in Mississippi and Alabama—mobs as hostile and hate-filled as I've seen in Chicago."[28]

There was, of course, the civil rights movement and the 1964 Civil Rights Act. But without a black perspective to correct it, these developments could foster the illusion among whites that the struggle for racial justice had ended in victory, even though there were still a few mop-up battles to be fought here and there. Instead, even today,

> whether out of hostility, indifference or simple lack of knowledge, large numbers of white Americans incorrectly believe that blacks are as well off as whites in terms of their jobs, incomes, school, and health care. . . . In fact, government statistics show that blacks have narrowed the gap, but continue to lag significantly behind whites in employment, income, education, and access to health care.[29]

Integration as an Ideal

During the period from the end of the Civil War through the end of World War I, episcopal leadership on racial issues was, to say the least, lackluster. The popes and Vatican officials repeatedly tried to prod the U.S. bishops to take action regarding the plight of blacks, but the main results were half measures and foot dragging.[30] The reign of terror known as lynching thrived during this period, and Cardinal Gibbons published an essay decrying lynching,[31] but the bishops said and did little more than this.

While this record is regrettable, it is understandable, since most blacks still lived in the rural South, where Catholics were a small minority. Also, most black Christians were Protestant. No longer slaves, they naturally wanted to control their own churches, and the more congregational Protestant church polities permitted them to do just that.[32] The bishops were also struggling to cope with waves of European immigration. As noted above, their problem was not how to seek new sheep, but how to tend the flocks they had.

Where Catholics began to adopt integration as the ideal and goal to be achieved, it was understood to be the social implication of the Christian conviction that all people were children of God, equal in dignity and rights, no matter what their skin color. Catholics could also prove their patriotism by promoting integration. After the 1954 Supreme Court decision *Brown v. Board of Education*, which struck down the doctrine of "separate but equal," and the later Supreme Court decisions outlawing segregation on interstate transportation (thus leading to the Freedom Rides on interstate buses), a "good American" favored integration. The fight against segregation also strengthened the United States in its struggle against "godless Communism." Progress toward integration could refute the Communist claim that freedom was a sham in a nation dominated by capitalists who kept the workers, white and black, down.[33]

But the particular ways in which the church understood integration served to obstruct its progress and even to foster the racism that it was supposed to conquer. According to the prevailing wisdom of the time, race was not an independent factor and force in social relationships and conflicts. Instead, it was reducible to other factors, such as economics or psychology. According to this analysis, whites were prejudiced against blacks because they were poor and, therefore, saw blacks as economic competitors. Whites might also be racists on account of the narrowness of their education, the biases of their subculture, or some form of immaturity. In short, racism was framed as an affliction of individuals not a systemic social dysfunction.

Most important, in my view, was another element of the prevailing sociological consensus, the notion that the assimilation of blacks into the mainstream of American life would follow the same pattern as the assimilation of white immigrant groups, like the Irish, the Polish, and the Italians. This prognosis acknowledged no distinctive features of black history that might retard this assimilation or even prevent it altogether. Futhermore, assimilation (in other words, integration) would take place automatically as a kind of natural process. No special remediation was needed for the brutalities of slavery, Jim Crow, lynching, and the Great Migration. The passage of time would produce the solution to racial conflict,[34] a notion that Martin Luther King Jr. later dismantled so effectively and eloquently in his classic "Letter from Birmingham City Jail," which was addressed to white *clergymen*, including the auxiliary bishop of Mobile-Birmingham.

White Catholics who embraced integration as an ideal also marginalized the distinctive history of black suffering. Progressives often did not want to hear about black history, to heed black voices, to take account of black experiences because this emphasis on the distinctiveness of the black experience in America seemed to reestablish the kind of difference that could justify separation— and from there, it could be a short step backward into segregation.

The painful consequences of this approach to integration can be seen in the story of the Federated Colored Catholics, told in sum by Cyprian Davis and in full by Marilyn Nickels.[35] The organization's founder, Thomas Wyatt Turner, came to prominence after World War I. At this time, Rome had begun pressing the American hierarchy about the plight of U.S. blacks and not least about the twenty-five race riots that had bloodied U.S. streets in just one year (1919). With his doctorate from Cornell and his professorship at Howard University, Turner was determined to improve the position of blacks in the U.S. Catholic Church.

Turner wrote to the apostolic delegate in November 1919 with a twenty-page statement of the Committee for the Advancement of Colored Catholics, which he had also sent to all the bishops prior to their first annual meeting. In this document Turner complained about the practice of making pastoral plans for blacks while not encouraging and supporting them in becoming agents of their own advancement: "It can be readily seen that effective work can be done among no people when it leaves that people out of the conferences and off the advisory boards which make plans for them."[36]

The bishops were unresponsive. The pastoral letter that emerged from their meeting was utterly inadequate in light of the race-based violence afflicting the country. It showed the truth of Turner's complaint that black Catholics had no voice in their church. To give them a voice, Turner's organization became the Federated Colored Catholics in 1924. Its members made it their business to write to the bishops each year in advance of the annual meeting, and they gave promise of enabling black Catholics to take their rightful place in the church.

Eight years later, in 1932, a disastrous split developed in Turner's organization. This was the result of a dispute between Turner and two Jesuits, William Markoe and John LaFarge, over the organization's goals and strategies. Turner, its founder, saw the development of self-consciousness, pride, identity, and leadership among blacks as essential. Markoe, however, could not recognize blacks as leaders. Also, to him, an organization of black Catholics for black Catholics led by black Catholics smacked too much of the segregation that he had pledged to oppose. He set out to remake the federation into an interracial organization. For his part, LaFarge thought that interracial collaboration in interracial education was the way forward, not the black advocacy that Turner promoted.[37] Nor could LaFarge be content to let Turner lead the way.

By 1932 LaFarge and Markoe had recruited enough allies to revise the federation's constitution in accord with their vision and to remove Turner as its president. The result was two groups, one led by Turner and the other by LaFarge, both weakened and less effectual. Cyprian Davis generously concedes that both Jesuits were great men, committed to the cause of black equality, but unable to understand why blacks had to appropriate their own history, secure their own identity, and find their own voice before integration could mean genuine harmony and not the repression of black distinctiveness and the loss of black gifts to the church.

Thus, the irony: LaFarge, who "saved the honor of Roman Catholicism in America by being the persistent voice of reason and justice in a time of apathy and racism,"[38] as well as other opponents of segregation, such as Markoe and Slattery,[39] actually held blacks back, for they had little sense that their black fellow Catholics had distinctive gifts to bring. Marginalizing Turner and his allies actually fostered racism, the very evil to which they were opposed. As LaFarge became the church's main voice on racism and Turner was effectively silenced, the implicit lesson was that a distinctive black identity either did not exist or was negligible. Thus, the ideal of integration absolved progressive white Catholics and theologians from listening to and learning from the experience and perspectives of blacks. When he later came to write his autobiography, *The Manner Is Ordinary*, LaFarge did not even mention Turner. For LaFarge and Markoe the Catholic song could only be sung if everyone sang the same notes at the same time—and, of course, a priest had to lead the choir. So Turner and his allies learned, long before Stokely Carmichael and Malcolm X warned about it, that integration in the wrong hands and heads meant black powerlessness.[40]

The Impact of Vatican II

During the period known as the Second Reconstruction, many Catholics stood and marched with the blacks who were demanding their rights. My own university—Loyola University, Chicago— holds a dubious place in U.S. Catholic history as the scene of the first demonstration by sign-carrying, habit-wearing nuns. They were protesting the Catholic Women's Club's "Whites Only" policy in maintaining a swimming pool on the university's downtown campus. But where were the theologians during the civil rights struggle? That is, where were our teachers during this time? And where were we?

We were all in libraries, classrooms, and lecture venues, trying to absorb and adjust to the new perspectives and emphases in theology and church life emerging from the Second Vatican Council. As Catholic theologians, we were preparing to promote the new initiatives that fidelity to the council demanded. As Joseph Komonchak reminds us:

> There are very few features of everyday Catholic life . . . that were not affected by the Council or at least by the changes said to have been introduced as a consequence or implementation of it. This is true both of the church's internal life and of its relationship to the "others": other Christians, other religions, unbelievers, "the world" in general. . . . The church had changed more in a decade than it had in the previous century: "The Church of Pius XII was closer to that of Pius IX than to that of Paul VI."[41]

Catching up meant, first of all, assimilating the council's sixteen documents and, in particular, its four constitutions. Our red-covered paperback translations of the council's Latin texts, with the gold medallion profiles of John XXIII and Paul VI on the cover, got pretty dog-eared during these years. So too did works by the European architects and interpreters of the council: bishops like Suenens, König, and Montini; and theologians like Rahner, Congar, Schillebeeckx, Tavard, and Ratzinger, who had generated the conciliar perspectives. At the same time, "catching up" meant engaging the work of non-Catholic Christian theologians, seeking to understand these separated fellow Christians on their own terms. It also meant efforts to become familiar with Judaism and the other religious traditions of the world.

As if all this were not enough, we also had to develop a new breed of Catholic theologian, the lay theologian. We had to carve out a place for theology in new locations, Catholic colleges and universities, and, in those settings, to transform theology into an academic discipline. No longer could theologians be content to provide high-octane catechesis or handy one-liners that a busy priest could use to put off intellectually curious Catholics.

And, as if all this were still not enough, the church looked to its theologians to develop a theology that reflected the particular experiences and gifts of the U.S. Roman Catholic Church. *Inculturation,* a new word for a new enterprise, appeared on theologians' agenda. What was demanded was no less than forging a new identity for the church in the United States. This was to be an identity crafted not *over against* but *in relation to* the "others"—other Christians, other religions, other cultures, and even the otherness of nonbelievers. Engagement with the "other" was now to be a permanent, constituent element of the Roman Catholic tradition in the United States.[42]

The inculturation agenda helps to answer the pained questions posed by James Cone and Bishop Joseph Francis: why were Catholic theologians so interested in Latin American liberation theology, even as they ignored our own homegrown liberation theology, meaning black theology?[43] After all, Cone's *Black Theology and Black Power* appeared in April 1969, just before Gutiérrez's *A Theology of Liberation*.

The answer is that we gravitated toward Latin American liberation theology because it was both indigenous and Catholic. As such, perhaps it offered clues and methods for grappling with the identity question that the council had created for the U.S. Church. As Deck has it:

> Liberation theology undoubtedly inspired real hope in many Catholics who belong to the generation that lived through the drama of the 1970s and 80s, the heady period of Vatican II reforms, the cold war and the worldwide, often violent human rights struggles of those tumultuous times. We found light in the methods and message of liberation theology, a compelling vision for an engaged and caring Christian praxis grounded in deep biblical and doctrinal currents.[44]

In short, the century's defining moment for the Roman Catholic Church, Vatican II, came precisely at a defining moment in the black struggle for justice in this country and during the birth and early years of black theology. Catholic theologians had good reasons to be preoccupied. Nor can we say that these issues of identity and mission have yet been resolved in such a way as to command a consensus.

Factors within Black Theology

We cannot overlook factors within black theology itself that complicated white theological efforts to engage it. The original matrix and stimulus for the development of black theology was the Black Power movement in 1966. Also, black separatism was a major theme stressed in black theology's earliest period.[45] Even if black theology was meant to be separate only temporarily—and it was, according to Cone[46]—it was still a separatism that seemed to absolve white theologians here and now from engaging it. Though black theologians insisted that the liberation they envisioned encompassed everyone, oppressed and oppressor alike, black theology was often presented as a theology for and by blacks only. But, as a "special interest" theology, whites could safely ignore it.[47] Cone's groundbreaking text *Black Theology and Black Power* could be mistaken simply as an effort to legitimize emerging black consciousness.

Moreover, a black theology written for and by blacks out of black experience looked like a theology with a short shelf life. As segregation died, black theology would naturally disappear. As blacks become integrated ("more like us"), the need for a black theology and the impulse to write it would fade away. Very few white readers perceived that the calls for black separation were actually efforts to establish a black-white theological dialogue, but on radically new grounds of equality.[48] Few white theologians heard the voices that said that blackness was not simply or even primarily a matter of skin color but of identifying with the struggle and sharing the suffering of the oppressed.[49]

Certainly, black anger and even hostility played a major role here, as Cone himself admits: "I must admit I was pretty hard on them and that partly accounts for their silence. But I was not going to pamper privileged Whites."[50] Cone is alluding to statements like the following, from *A Black Theology of Liberation*: "To whites who want to know what they can do (a favorite question of oppressors), Black Theology says, 'Keep your damn mouth closed, and let us black people get our thing together.'"[51]

Another problem for white academic theologians was how to interpret a theology drawn largely from nontraditional theological sources: sermons, hymns, devotions, and narratives. In *The Spirituals and the Blues* (1972), Cone had maintained that "'academic tools' are not enough. The interpreter must feel the Spirit; that is, he must feel his way into the power of black music, responding to both its rhythm and the faith in experience it affirms."[52] No mean feat, this.

A third difficulty is white Catholic theologians' unfamiliarity and even discomfort with the non-sacramental, Bible-based, free-church traditions of most black churches, the root and home of black theology. The charismatic, spontaneous styles of black Christian worship and leadership contrasted mightily with the sedate, structured style of Catholic liturgy and ordained ministry.

Also, these churches were not Catholic, and the Roman Catholic Church had deemed itself to be the one and only true church of Christ for four and a half centuries. As George Tavard has observed, when it came to ecumenism, Vatican II initiated a tradition; it did not articulate and advance a development already under way, as was the case with the liturgical renewal. Not until November 1964 did the church declare that "we must come to know the mind [*animum*] of our separated brothers [*fratrum*]" (*Unitatis Redintegratio*, 9) and call for a corresponding theological renewal.

Finally, there was the "fragmentary" character of black theology that seemed to fall short of "real" theology as an ordered, systematic exposition of the whole of revelation. The term *systematic theology* is falling into disuse, but the aspiration that it expresses still lives and controls Catholic theology's norms and expectations. From Vatican I's notion of theology as an imperfect understanding of truths in relation to one another in 1869 to John Paul II's *Fides et Ratio* in 1998, there is real continuity. But, as David Tracy says:

> No major African American thinker, long before the rest of us, ever attempted or wanted a system. They have left us, all of them (especially James Cone in his theology, Cornel West in his philosophy, and Toni Morrison in her literature) with something far more valuable than a system. They have left to us fragments that break and undo such pretense to totality, and that describe hints and guesses of hope . . . fragmentary glimpses of light and redemption. These are the crucial resources which African-American thought, if heeded, can provide for our dessicated public realm.[53]

So there are many good reasons for white Catholic theologians to have marginalized black theology. But these reasons are "good" in the sense of *explanatory*, not "good" in the sense of *exculpatory*, not good enough to refute the charge of racism, however nonviolent our racism has been. The reasons are not good enough because they have led to our failure in solidarity, as Copeland describes it, "the empathetic incarnation of Christian love [that] . . . entails the recognition of the humanity of the 'other' as humanity, along with regard for the 'other' in her (and his) own otherness."[54] And the reasons are not good enough because systemic white Catholic theological racism threatens our credentials. Our failure in solidarity means that we have failed in significant ways to live up to our vocation as Catholic theologians.

Conclusion

A substantial and critical engagement with black theology is indispensable to the vocation and identity of U.S. Catholic theologians. Just as we are familiar and engaged with Latin American liberation theology and feminist theology, as well as the various challenges that can be grouped under the rubric of post-modernity, just as much and so much more must we embrace black theology as an indispensable dialogue partner. Catholic theology, in order to be truly *Catholic* theology in the United States, must be worked out in conversation with black theology. If black theology remains as marginal as it now is, then our claim to be Catholic theologians can be rightly challenged. In reflecting on "The Social Context of American Catholic Theology," Canadian Gregory Baum found much to praise, but wondered, "Is American theology . . . generated out of an identification with the middle class?"[55] When we realize that one of the best books on black theology, Theo Witvliet's *The Way of the Black Messiah: The Hermeneutical Challenge of Black Theology* (1987), was written by a Dutch scholar, translated by an Englishman, and published by an obscure printing house, and is now out of print, we realize that Baum is on to something.

As long as black theology is off our radar screens, we can be accused of subverting Vatican II. We can be charged with exploiting the council as a way to buttress our own prejudices and privileges rather than embracing it as the new Pentecost for which Blessed John XXIII prayed. We may even be dismissed as an effete elite, little more than chaplains to "sick middle-class egos," in James Cone's typically forceful phrasing.[56]

I know these are strong claims. Let me try to back them up.

J. Bryan Hehir has explained how the council moved the social justice agenda of the church from its periphery to its center. Prior to Vatican II, he says, "Social ministry was understood (or tolerated) as an *extension* of the Church's life, but not always seen as decisively something *of the Church's nature.*"[57] And in commenting on his reading of *Dignitatis Humanae* and *Gaudium et Spes*, Hehir writes, "The decisive conciliar contribution to the social and public ministry of the Church was to locate the defense of the human person at the center of Catholic ecclesiology, thereby moving the social ministry from the periphery to the core of the Church's life and work."[58]

Not only was the church's public ministry reconceived, but so also were the ministers, who were to be the principal agents in the service of the person. These belonged to the local church. As we know, "the local church" is prominent among the council's retrievals from the church's past to renew her in the present. When the Catholic Theological Society of America focused on the theme of "The Local Church," Komonchak emphasized that

> this Church is not only made manifest and visible in dioceses and local congregations; it is represented there, in the strong sense of this word. The council's statements are strong and direct: The one and universal Church is gathered together in such churches; it is present and active in them; it is built up and grows in them; it is in them and out of them that it exists; and, for all these reasons, the local gatherings of believers are rightly called "churches." As a number of commentators have pointed out, this vision represents something like a Copernican revolution in ecclesiology.[59]

Thus, Vatican II maintains that of its very nature the church must be substantially engaged in the world to protect and advance the transcendent dignity of the person. It also restores to its proper place the meaning and mission of the church, as it is realized and actualized in eucharistic communities, parishes, dioceses, and larger groupings, like regional and national conferences.

Hehir rightly identifies the striking conjunction of these two themes in Paul VI's *Octogesima Adveniens* (1971), where the Holy Father says:

> There is of course a wide diversity among the situations in which Christians—willingly or unwillingly—find themselves according to regions, socio-political systems and cultures. . . . In the face of such widely varying situations it is difficult for us to utter a unified message and to put forward a solution which has universal validity. Such is not our ambition, nor is it our mission. *It is up to the Christian communities to analyze with objectivity the situation which is proper to their own country*, to shed on it the light of the Gospel's unalterable words and to draw principles of reflection, norms of judgment and directives for action from the social teaching of the Church.[60] (Emphasis added.)

Now what is being described here, if not the work of theology? And who is to do it, if not we who call ourselves Catholic theologians? And hadn't the council already given theologians this mandate back in 1965, when it said that "it is the task of the entire People of God, especially pastors and theologians, to hear, distinguish, and interpret the many voices of our age, and to judge them in light of the divine Word" (*Gaudium et Spes*, 44)?

But if theologians overlook slavery, Jim Crow, the ritualistic and systematic terrorizing of blacks known as lynching, and the devastating residue of these horrors that still poison our national life today, how can they possibly "analyze with objectivity the situation which is proper to their own country?" And how reliable can their theological reflection be if they try "to shed on it the light of the Gospel's unalterable words" without the help of the black theology that has arisen precisely out of black suffering and sorrow and endurance and triumph?

Theologians could do worse than to heed James Cone: "Begin the antiracist struggle where you are. . . . One of the most important things whites can do in fighting white supremacy is to support black empowerment in the society, church and theology. . . . The black church and black theology are black empowerment in religion."[61] To begin where you are means to resolve, here and now, to make an end of white Catholic theological racism, and to take our black Christian sisters and brothers just as seriously as we have taken our other dialogue partners. To the extent that we do, we will vindicate the claim to be Catholic theologians. We will be more faithful to our vocation as Catholic theologians. It is true, as Shawn Copeland reminds us, that "the cost of our own religious, moral, and intellectual conversion [is] steep." But who ever said that the vocation of the Catholic theologian was supposed to be easy?

W. E. B. Du Bois's classic work *The Souls of Black Folk* appeared over one hundred years ago. How little he would have to change to make his analyses just as accurate today as they were a century ago! The most famous line from his book is, of course, "The problem of the twentieth century is the problem of the color-line." Less well known is the prayer with which Du Bois ends his book. Let me make his prayer mine:

> Hear my cry, O God the Reader; vouchsafe that this my book fall not still-born into the world wilderness. Let there spring, Gentle One, from out its leaves vigor of thought and thoughtful deed to reap the harvest wonderful. Let the ears of a guilty people tingle with truth, and seventy millions sigh for the righteousness which exalteth nations, in this drear day when human brotherhood is mockery and a snare. Thus in Thy good time may infinite reason turn the tangle straight, and these crooked marks on a fragile leaf be not indeed.

Notes

[1] M. Shawn Copeland, "Racism and the Vocation of the Theologian," *Spiritus* 2, no. 1 (Spring 2002): 16.

[2] James H. Cone, "Looking Back, Going Forward: Black Theology as Public Theology," in *Black Faith and Public Talk: Critical Essays on James H. Cone's* Black Theology and Black Power, ed. Dwight N. Hopkins (Maryknoll, NY: Orbis Books, 1999), 257.

[3] James H. Cone, "Black Liberation Theology and Black Catholics: A Critical Conversation," *Theological Studies* 61, no. 4 (2000): 732.

[4] Cone, "Black Liberation Theology and Black Catholics," 737.

[5] Jamie T. Phelps, "Communion Ecclesiology and Black Liberation Theology," *Theological Studies* 61, no. 4 (2000): 692.

[6] Cited in Cone, "Looking Back, Going Forward," 253.

[7] See, among others, Kenneth M. Stampp, *The Peculiar Institution: Slavery in the Ante-Bellum South* (New York: Vintage, 1956); and Norman R. Yetman, ed., *Voices from Slavery* (New York: Holt, Rinehart and Winston, 1970).

[8] Cornel West, "Black Theology and Human Identity," in Hopkins, *Black Faith and Public Talk*, 16. See also Philip Dray, *At the Hands of Persons Unknown: The Lynching of Black America* (New York: Random House, 2002).

[9] Johann Baptist Metz, "Unterwegs zu einer Christologie nach Auschwitz," *Stimmen der Zeit* 218, no. 11 (November 2000): 755–60. On Metz's conversion, see Gregory Baum, *Compassion and Solidarity: The Church for Others* (Concord, MA: Anansi, 1987), 78–80.

[10] James Boggs, *Racism and the Class Struggle* (New York: Monthly Review Press, 1970), 147–48.

[11] For brevity's sake here, I follow Dwight N. Hopkins and include womanist theology within black theology. Of course, womanist theology, which emerged in the mid-1980s, is not simply a subcategory of black theology. While it owes much of its inspiration to black theology (and to feminist theology), womanist theologians critique any theology, white or black, that is blind to the distinctive sufferings and strengths of women of color. See Dwight N. Hopkins, *Introducing Black Theology of Liberation* (Maryknoll, NY: Orbis Books, 1999), 125–56; Stephanie Y. Mitchem, *Introducing Womanist Theology* (Maryknoll, NY: Orbis Books, 2002).

[12] Cone, "Black Liberation Theology and Black Catholics," 741.

[13] Bryan Massingale, "The African American Experience and U.S. Roman Catholic Ethics: 'Strangers and Aliens No Longer?'" in *Black and Catholic: The Challenge and Gift of Black Folk*, ed. Jamie T. Phelps (Milwaukee: Marquette University Press, 1997), 81–86.

[14] Preston N. Williams, "Religious and Social Aspects of Roman Catholic and Black American Relationships," *Proceedings of the Catholic Theological Society of America* 28 (1973): 15–30.

[15] Joseph R. Nearon, "Preliminary Report. Research Committee for Black Theology," *Proceedings of the Catholic Theological Society of America* 29 (1974): 413.

[16] Ibid., 415.

[17] Cone, "Black Liberation Theology and Black Catholics," 741.

[18] Karl Rahner, "Dimensions of Martyrdom: A Plea for the Broadening of a Classical Concept," in *Martyrdom Today*, ed. Johannes Baptist Metz and Edward Schillebeeckx (New York: Seabury, 1983), 9–11.

[19] Chester Gillis, *Roman Catholicism in America* (New York: Columbia University Press, 1999), 59.

[20] Ibid., 61.

[21] Bryan T. Froehle and Mary L. Gautier, *Catholicism USA. A Portrait of the Catholic Church in the United States* (Maryknoll, NY: Orbis Books, 2000), 8.

[22] John A. McDermott, as quoted in John T. McGreevy, *Parish Boundaries: The Catholic Encounter with Race in the Twentieth-Century Urban North* (Chicago: University of Chicago Press, 1996), 132.

[23] See Darlene Clark Hine, William C. Hine, and Stanley Harrold, *The African-American Odyssey* (Upper Saddle River, NJ: Prentice Hall, 2000), 383.

[24] McGreevy, *Parish Boundaries*, 139. For a sympathetic outsider's view of Roman Catholicism's assimilationist bent, see Edward Farley, *Divine Empathy: A Theology of God* (Minneapolis: Fortress Press, 1996), 260–61.

[25] Dennis Geaney, quoted in McGreevy, *Parish Boundaries*, 190.

[26] McGreevy, *Parish Boundaries*, 110.

[27] Bryan N. Massingale, "The Ethics of Racism," *Origins* 28, no. 4 (November 26, 1998): 425.

[28] Martin Luther King Jr., in Stephen B. Oates, *Let the Trumpet Sound: A Life of Martin Luther King, Jr.* (New York: HarperPerennial, 1994), 413.

[29] Richard Morin, "It's Not as It Seems," *Washington Post National Weekly Edition* (July 16–22, 2001), 34.

[30] Cyprian Davis, *The History of Black Catholics in the United States* (New York: Crossroad Publications, 1990), 216–17.

[31] Cardinal Gibbons, "Lynch Law: Its Causes and Remedy," *North American Review* 181 (October 1905): 502–9.

[32] Eric Foner, *Reconstruction: America's Unfinished Revolution, 1863–1877* (New York: Harper and Row, 1988), 81, 91–92.

[33] C. Vann Woodward, *The Strange Career of Jim Crow*, 3rd rev. ed. (New York: Oxford University Press, 1974), 130–32.

[34] Michael Omi and Howard Winant, *Racial Formation in the United States from the 1960s to the 1980s* (New York: Routledge and Kegan Paul, 1986), 10–23.

[35] Davis, *The History of Black Catholics in the United States*, 214–29; Marilyn Nickels, *Black Catholic Protest and the Federated Colored Catholics, 1917–1933: Three Perspectives on Racial Justice* (New York: Garland Publishing, 1988).

[36] Thomas Wyatt Turner, as quoted in Davis, *The History of Black Catholics in the United States*, 219.

[37] John LaFarge, *The Catholic Viewpoint on Race Relations* (Garden City, NY: Hanover House-Doubleday, 1956), 45, 61.

[38] Davis, *The History of Black Catholics in the United States*, 228.

[39] Joseph A. Brown, *To Stand on the Rock: Meditations on Black Catholic Identity* (Maryknoll, NY: Orbis Books, 1998), 150–51.

[40] On LaFarge and Markoe, see also McGreevy, *Parish Boundaries*, 38–47. This inadequate approach to racial justice continues today in the Church. "Catholic teaching on racism tends to speak about and for aggrieved African Americans, but seldom reflects, acknowledges, or encourages Black thought, initiative, or leadership" (Bryan N. Massingale, "James Cone and Recent Catholic Episcopal Teaching on Racism," *Theological Studies* 61 [2000]: 723).

[41] Joseph A. Komonchak, "Interpreting the Council: Catholic Attitudes toward Vatican II," in *Being Right: Conservative Catholics in America*, ed. Mary Jo Weaver and R. Scott Appleby (Bloomington: Indiana University Press, 1995), 17. For a sociological account of this impact, see Roger Finke and Rodney Stark, *The Churching of America 1776–1990* (New Brunswick, NJ: Rutgers University Press, 1992).

[42] "In three respects at least, the Council posed major threats to the self-articulation of modern Catholicism: by its far more positive assessment of modernity in its political and cultural features, by its call for an updating and reform of Church practice in the light of modernity, and by its appeal to particular and local churches to assume responsibility for culturally distinct realizations of Catholic Christianity" (Joseph A. Komonchak, "The Ecclesial and Cultural Roles of Theology," *Proceedings of the Catholic Theological Society of America* [1985]: 23).

[43] James H. Cone, "A Theological Challenge of the American Catholic Church," in *Speaking the Truth: Ecumenism, Liberation, and Black Theology* (Maryknoll, NY: Orbis Books, 1999), 51. Bishop

Francis is quoted in Massingale, "James Cone and Recent Catholic Episcopal Teaching on Racism," 701–2.

[44] Allan Figueroa Deck, "Beyond *La Pausa*: Liberation Theologies Live," *America*, February 3, 2003, 20–21.

[45] James H. Cone, *For My People: Black Theology and the Black Church* (Maryknoll, NY: Orbis Books, 1984), 19.

[46] Ibid., 42.

[47] Peter J. Paris, "Comparing the Public Theologies of James H. Cone and Martin Luther King, Jr." in Hopkins, *Black Faith and Public Talk*, 218.

[48] Theo Witvliet, *The Way of the Black Messiah*, trans. John Bowden (Oak Park, IL: Meyer-Stone Books, 1987), 131–32.

[49] Diana L. Hayes, "Through the Eyes of Faith: The Seventh Principle of the *Nguzo Saba* and the Beatitudes of Matthew," in *Taking Down Our Harps: Black Catholics in the United States*, ed. Diana L. Hayes and Cyprian Davis (Maryknoll, NY: Orbis Books, 1998), 62.

[50] James H. Cone, "Theology's Great Sin: Silence in the Face of White Supremacy," *Union Seminary Quarterly Review* 55, nos. 3–4 (2001): 9–10.

[51] James H. Cone, *A Black Theology of Liberation* (Philadelphia: Lippincott, 1970), 194; see also Cone, *For My People*, 31–52.

[52] James H. Cone, as quoted in Brown, *To Stand on the Rock*, 52.

[53] David Tracy, "African American Thought: The Discovery of Fragments," in Hopkins, *Black Faith and Public Talk*, 37–38.

[54] M. Shawn Copeland, "The New Anthropological Subject at the Heart of the Mystical Body of Christ," *Proceedings of the Catholic Theological Society of America* 53 (1998): 36–37.

[55] Gregory Baum, "The Social Context of American Catholic Theology," *Proceedings of the Catholic Theological Society of America* 41 (1986): 94.

[56] James H. Cone, "The White Church and Black Power," in *Black Theology: A Documentary History*, vol. 1, 2nd rev. ed., ed. James H. Cone and Gayraud S. Wilmore (Maryknoll, NY: Orbis Books, 1993), 78. This is an excerpt from *Black Theology and Black Power*, 1969.

[57] J. Bryan Hehir, "Church-State and Church-World: The Ecclesiological Implications," *Proceedings of the Catholic Theological Society of America* 41 (1986): 56.

[58] Ibid., 58.

[59] Joseph A. Komonchak, "Ministry and the Local Church," *Proceedings of the Catholic Theological Society of America* 36 (1981): 58.

[60] Paul VI, *Octogesima Adveniens,* as quoted in Hehir, "Church-State and Church-World," 59–60.

[61] Cone, "Theology's Great Sin," 13.

2

· · · ·

WHITE ECONOMIC
AND EROTIC DISEMPOWERMENT

A Theological Exploration
in the Struggle against Racism

Mary Elizabeth Hobgood

White theologians need a variety of theoretical approaches in the intellectual and political struggle against racism. For a start, I suggest a critical study of white overprivilege complemented by an exploration of white disempowerment.

Whites are accountable for understanding how racism advantages them at the expense of others. This is a relatively recent turn in the exploration of white racism, which typically has focused on how non-white communities are economically exploited, politically oppressed, and culturally marginalized. However, there is no subordination without a complementary exercise of domination. Whites have the responsibility to interrogate and resist whiteness as a social location of unjust structured advantage.[1] Indeed, the last decades have seen a proliferation of explorations about white racial advantage, especially by feminist scholars from diverse communities of color.[2]

Exploring the ubiquitous, and for whites often invisible, aspects of white advantage is a lifelong task of gaining religious awareness and engaging moral action. I call this awareness religious in light of the fact that the word *religion* comes from the Latin *religio*, meaning "a moral bond." Awareness of white privilege is religious because it deals with discerning how intimately world-minority white affluent people are bound up with world-majority communities of color. However, the quality of this binding together of overprivileged and underprivileged groups is unjust, demanding of us both resistance and transformation. Interdependence should be honored within just or right relations, but the reality is that world-majority people are impoverished. Some are white, but most are not. A structural analysis of the global economy reveals that poor people provide the affluent minority with what it needs not only to sustain life but to live in luxury. Without the blood, sweat, tears, and political disempowerment endured by the underfed, overworked, and often homeless world majority, affluent whites would lack monopolized access to better paying jobs and the relatively cheap accouterments and services of the good life—and also likely be hungry, unshod, and unclothed. The deepest possible religious awareness is for us to "feel our own flesh as vital and vulnerable" and to be aware of our dependence on others.[3]

This essay, however, does not focus on the ongoing responsibility of whites to interrogate whiteness as a location of systemic, structured advantage. Rather, I wish to focus on an equally important but until recently neglected area in the struggle against racism. I wish to consider how white supremacy camouflages the exploitation of many whites themselves within the interlocking social systems of a racist, capitalist political economy. Racism functions as a safety valve in a society that delivers less and less to most whites. Attention to the overprivilege of whites must be supplemented by an exploration of how racism upholds status for the majority of light-skinned people, even while their own well-being is continually eroding in a downwardly mobile economy. Whiteness actually disadvantages many, if not most, whites even as it advantages some, especially an affluent 20 percent. Coming to terms with the immorality of racism cannot be fully discerned without paying attention to the construction of racism as a mirror image of the exploitation of most white people.

Disempowerment Coexists with Overprivilege

In arguing that white disempowerment is a legitimate focus for exploring white supremacy, I offer two quotations for consideration. The first is a well-known saying of the Boston-based Combahee River Collective, a politically active group in the 1970s. It claimed: "The most profound and potentially most radical politics comes directly out of our own identity, as opposed to working to end somebody else's oppression."[4] The second quotation is what Saint Matthew's Gospel calls the greatest commandment: "You shall love the Lord your God with all your heart, and with all your soul, and with all your mind. . . . You shall love your neighbor as yourself" (Mt 22:37, 39). The source of the most radical politics is our obligation to work for our own liberation. The energy for political transformation comes from the deepest core of our being and is driven by authentic self-love. Deep compassion for ourselves is the basis for true love of neighbor, and love of neighbor is essential for our own well-being.

In contrast, capitalist culture creates isolated consumers who persist in believing the myth of the individual and who live in communities segregated by class and race. White, affluent, capitalist people by and large are preoccupied with their personal consumption levels, not the condition of the larger community. Therefore, morality is viewed as relating well to others who more often than not share a similar social location. Since biblical love and meaningful political action depend on making the connection between our well-being and that of other social groups, white, affluent people in capitalist societies are at a disadvantage with respect to discerning ethical social relations.

Moreover, believing the myth that people are individuals without need of others makes it easy to think that loving others must be done at the expense of one's self. To suggest that loving others well can emanate only from authentic self-love and interdependence with others is viewed as either selfish or compromised. This ethical orientation is pejoratively labeled enlightened self-interest. Working on behalf of one's authentic self-interest is assumed to be not only different from but also morally inferior to "selfless" altruism. Supposedly the highest form of morality requires that other-love be radically divorced from love of self and, indeed, must be done at the expense of self.

Our religious heritage disagrees. The ancient Jewish tradition that informed Jesus is full of human wisdom affirmed today in many quarters, from feminist theory (the self is fundamentally relational and radically interdependent) to psychotherapy (being loved teaches one to love one's self and is the basis of love of others). *We recognize the needs of others to the degree that we recognize our own.* Psychology claims that true love of self is the opposite of narcissism or egocentric obsession with the self, which comes from *lack* of self love. Only when authentic self-love exists is other-love possible and the basis for genuine solidarity present. Only when we appreciate our radical interdependence on others and the more-than-human world can we critique the Western dualism of self-love and other-love. Therefore, to create a moral world, including a world without racism, the fundamental requirement of healthy self-love cannot be stressed enough. I agree with my womanist colleagues that we should approach any adulation of traditional altruism with a hermeneutic of suspicion, because most notions of self-sacrifice in our tradition are based on a self/other antagonism, whether the dominant/subordinate or the helper/helpee split so characteristic of oppressive Western dualistic thought.[5]

My thesis is that racism emanates from and is perpetuated by the disability of whites to be authentically self-loving. In a society that rejects basic human needs and attributes, racism is the projection of white self-alienation. The capitalist political economy must be racist so that the white majority, no matter how economically vulnerable, ignorant, or tempted to crime, will believe it is made up of industrious, knowledgeable, virtuous, and law-abiding folks who are better than those non-white "others." Whites need racism in order to rest assured that those "not like us" embody what whites have rejected in themselves. Most important, U.S. society must be racist so the white majority will comply with the work and sexual requirements of the capitalist machine. As critical theorist Ian Haney Lopez suggests, whites may receive very few returns and lay claim to only a very short stick in the political economy, but with the help of white racial supremacy they manage to maintain some self-esteem. One can be an enthusiastic supporter of the status quo, even one that is doing you in, if whiteness validates at every turn that others, not you, are lazy, stupid, lascivious, or criminal.[6] Racism gives those constructed as white a set of comforting identities, often at odds with their actual social reality. Indeed, economically poor whites who conform to the dominant norms are needed to "prove" that impoverishment can be endured without resorting to crime. Above all, racism provides scapegoats for angry, frustrated whites who remain mystified as to the real source of their problems.

People of color have long realized these insights,[7] but whites need to keep fleshing out this knowledge for their own edification. In a culture inattentive to physical, emotional, and spiritual needs, whites project the hatred and discomfort about their own unacknowledged bodily needs onto diverse communities of color who, in the process, become overly identified with their bodies. Self-hatred of white embodiment is manifested in a myriad of ways, including apathy about the human need to control labor and do meaningful work; powerlessness about economic stagnation and the inability to influence major decisions that impact lives; shame about sexual desire, leisure, and play; and fear of vulnerability to sickness, aging, and death. In short, white ambivalence about embodiment is at play in the inhuman ways individuals and institutions treat children, the elderly, the disabled, the unemployed and underemployed, and people from diverse communities of color. Until whites realize how they rely on racism to manage their own fear and alienation, they will lack both the theoretical basis necessary for rejecting racism as well as the passionate energy to work effectively against it.

If biblical insights, as well as political wisdom, about the primacy of self-love in just social relations are true, if the politics of justice comes from an awareness of the need for liberation, then exploring how white supremacy is damaging to whites becomes an essential ingredient of any serious theological and ethical approach to transforming racism. With theologian Bryan Massingale, I agree that the "poverty of moral suasion" is unable to generate a political movement adequate for dismantling racism.[8] Quoting James Cone, Massingale points out that "an appeal to . . . moral guilt" about racism relies "too little on the tools of social analysis."[9] I would add that a politics of moral suasion is ineffective because it lacks a feminist and womanist critique of the self/other split, as well as sex/gender, race, and class analyses. When armed with such resources, it becomes possible to examine not only the suffering of diverse communities of color under racism but also *the root of this suffering in whites' own alienation.* On this score I call particular attention to economic and erotic alienation and the ways in which racism manages, expresses, and extends it. This critical knowledge is crucial because the depth of our alienation marks the depth of our self-hatred, and the absence of self-love generates the white pathology that spews upon others through the insidious channels of both institutional and personal racism. White people, even otherwise well educated and affluent white people, who fail to come to terms with their own relative oppression under racism will be of little help to their sisters and brothers of color, who have much more to fear from this system of moral evil.

For whites to confront racism, they must own this work as a matter of their own liberation. This entails recognizing at least two ways in which racism manages white discomfort with embodiment. The first way is by controlling anger and frustration at economic vulnerability, which continues to be the lot of most whites in the class system.

Racism Manages White Economic Disempowerment

Contrary to common North American assumptions about the ubiquity of upward mobility, most whites have been and will remain stagnant or downwardly mobile in a capitalist political economy, and racism helps manage white anger and fear, given this economic reality. Racism performs this function today much as it did when whiteness was invented in the eighteenth century. In his 1997 *The Invention of the White Race*, historian Theodore Allen argues that in colonial America no one understood themselves as "not white." At that time there was no racialized conception of the social subject. (It is important to savor this fact and imagine a world without racism, which actually existed historically.)

After indigenous people were driven off the land or exterminated, there were two classes in America: the wealthy European planter class and the class of bonded servants. Bonded laborers were of both African and European origin, but this difference was all but inconsequential in light of their common servitude and harsh treatment. Whether of African or European roots, bonded laborers produced the raw products that fueled the Industrial Revolution and generated the wealth of the early capitalist class in England and the colonies. Their work never ended because, under capitalism, products are valued not so much for their usefulness as for their capacity to make a profit in a world of expanding trade.

In an earlier 1940s study, *Capitalism and Slavery*, Afro-Caribbean scholar Eric Williams documents how poor English and Irish men, women, and children were kidnapped, as were Africans, for a middle-passage journey to the Americas. Ample historical evidence exists that in the seventeenth century the conditions of poor English and Irish indentured servants were largely the same as those who arrived from Africa. In these early years many European bonded laborers, like most Africans, died before they were freed.[10]

Like Williams, Theodore Allen argues that modern racism did not exist in seventeenth-century America and that there was little difference in the treatment of African and European bonded servants. In addition, Allen analyzes the strong bonds of affection between African and European laborers. Diverse origins or no, these people cared for and stood up for one another.[11]

Meanwhile, in order to make increasing profits for themselves, the colonial planter class monopolized productive land ownership along the eastern seaboard, as the upper classes had in England. This meant that most indentured servants had no means of a livelihood, even if they survived the period of servitude. Consequently, the small planter class was faced with the growing hostility of a newly freed but disenfranchised class of people who faced a destitute future and yet retained strong bonds with those Europeans and Africans they had left behind on the plantations.

Bacon's Rebellion in 1676 Virginia was a key example of what the planter class was up against. Bacon's Rebellion was a revolt of bonded laborers and the newly freed destitute—six thousand European Americans and two thousand African Americans—who wanted not only emancipation from servitude but also freedom to own productive land and turn plantation monoculture America into a diversified smallholder economy.[12] Clearly, from the capitalists' point of view, something had to be done to divide this huge and potentially revolutionary class. In his study Allen shows that from the end of the seventeenth century and throughout the eighteenth, the economic elite carefully engineered a system of white privilege. During this time the period of European servitude was shortened while African servitude was lengthened to a lifetime. Such advantages, granted only to those of European heritage, increased the propensity of European bonded servants to spy on Africans before they were freed. It also allowed newly freed Europeans limited access to farmland if they did militia duty—the origin of the American police—to provide social surveillance on behalf of the planter class. The emerging system of white privilege and protection broke down the ties of affection and solidarity that had developed among the various bonded laborers and redirected the anger of impoverished and degraded whites. A buffer class of poor Europeans, both indentured and emancipated, received the psychological wages of whiteness as long as they served the interests of the small economic elite.

This dynamic continues today. Those who own and control land, labor, and resources remain a very small sector of the U.S. population, which is now approaching 300 million people. Drawing on 1995 statistics, economist Michael Zweig observes that only those who run 16,000 of the 225 million U.S. businesses exercise real power in the U.S. political economy. They are the people who decide, for example, what we produce (like bombs or daycare centers), how we produce it (in ways that weaken or empower workers), and how the profits are reinvested in the economy. The interlocking directorates among these largest corporations as well as the largest banks form the core of the U.S. ruling class, which, Zweig writes, would not overflow Yankee Stadium, which holds fifty-seven thousand people.[13]

To see why racism remains important for the capitalist class, consider that the lower-income sector of the U.S. working class constitutes over 60 percent of the labor force.[14] Almost half of the lower working class is composed of white men, who in the last thirty years have lost 20 percent of their share of society's income. (The workers in the lowest fifth of the working class lost

14 percent). These workers are downwardly mobile but do not qualify for programs that benefit the 20 percent of workers below them.[15]

Many realize that investors make super profits off the low-wage labor of people of color, but that is not all. Although whites, particularly white men, monopolize the capitalist class and upper-income jobs, as economist Doug Henwood notes, "there is no shortage of awful jobs for white folks either."[16] Even more to the point, when you are white, male, and downwardly mobile, and when you lack a critical analysis of the class system, what excuses do you have for your failure to succeed? Not many. And so it is easy to be compliant with the system of racist scapegoating in order to explain your eroding status and lack of real privilege.

Given capitalist dynamics, therefore, racism is not a flaw in the system. Racism is not a problem to be solved. Rather, *racism is and always has been a brilliant solution to the frustration of most working whites in the U.S. class system.* Current racist measures, such as welfare dismantling, the expanding white racist militia movement, and the takeover of government by the white evangelical movement and political right wing, help manage the frustration and increasing economic vulnerability of the white majority who need some group to blame their troubles on—as long as it is not the capitalist class. As it was in the seventeenth century, so it is now. Racism continues, not primarily because we have inherited it from the past, but because the political economy still needs it to give downwardly mobile whites some status and to divide the working class. Theodore Allen ends his study by asking: How long until upper-income working class whites (whose economic vulnerability is also rapidly increasing as more formerly upper-income jobs become micromanaged, "deskilled," outsourced, downsized, and untenured) realize how whiteness is used against them by obstructing the class solidarity necessary for economic transformation?

Racism Manages White Erotic Disempowerment

A second way racism hurts whites is by deepening the erotic disempowerment of white people. The racial system demands self-alienating personal qualities and the distortion of feelings in order to achieve the status of whiteness. These attributes include being a workaholic and overly rational in one's general approach to life and, ostensibly, adhering to a highly restricted sexual ethic. To achieve white racial status, people are expected to experience erotic desire as shameful and the desire to avoid pain as weakness. To maintain white racial status one must generally live as if pleasure is bad and pain is good. Under capitalism, workers are rewarded for grinding away long hours and being obsessed with work. At the same time, most have little control over their work, and those with some autonomy are rapidly losing it. (Consider what has happened to physicians, for example, under the profit-making HMOs.) Under capitalism no sector of the working class controls the work process or the profits made from its work.

Alienated work necessitates alienated sexuality. Historian Thomas Holt argues that in the nineteenth century African-Jamaican freed people initially rejected the assumption that they would move naturally into the slave wages of so-called free labor. After centuries of slavery they had their own ideas about how to expend their time and energy and how to organize social, political, and economic life. However, the elite minority could not keep profits up and at the same time accommodate the desires of former slaves for leisure, eroticism, and simple living exemplified by their house gardens and bartering among their communities. To become willing to work for capitalist wages, the newly emancipated had to be forced off the land, as had the English poor before them and as indigenous communities everywhere still are under contemporary capitalist imperialism. To work for wages, newly emancipated men were also forced into marriages with dependent wives and children and told to desire a proliferation of material goods. As Holt explains, even after they were "proletarianized" as proper workaholics and consumers, their sexual desire was further targeted in order to prevent equal participation with whites in civil society.[17]

As a consequence of the life-denying needs of capitalism, people of color can never be workaholic or erotophobic enough— at least never as much as those with white racial status. In the nineteenth century, racism further developed by demonizing emancipated blacks who might hold different ideas about work and sex, even as they, along with the fairer-skinned, were constructed into industrious, monogamous, and consumerist capitalist people. The creation of racism was also needed to discipline the majority of workers, who were white. When theologian Shawn Copeland writes that "to be Black is to incarnate negativity, criminality, to be what is foul, loathsome and repugnant," white people should see a mirror held up to their own faces.[18] What has been rendered negative, criminal, foul, loathsome, and repugnant is human vitality and vulnerability, which whites must reject in order to be white. People of color are constructed to represent and demonize all human desires opposed to the capitalist machine. Racism is the self-alienated projection of white people's fear of their own bodies, of monotonous work, of sexual hungers, and of susceptibility to sickness and death. *White people scapegoat those without white racial status because they do not want to take responsibility for their economic vulnerability, erotic desires, and fundamental mortality.* As theologian James Perkinson explains, whites use racism as "a buffer against the demands of maturity," as a way to avoid growing up.[19] He says that racism will only be overcome when the anxieties that require whiteness are overcome.[20]

Perkinson's argument is that white theology, with its quest for certainty and its patriarchal ethic of social control, has been used in the same way—as a way to avoid adult responsibility for our embodied lives. As we know only too well, the anti-body system of U.S. racism has had considerable support from Christianity and Greek philosophy. As J. Giles Milhaven has noted, the necessity of rising above bodily experience is repeated monotonously in the classical theologies of "Origen, Augustine, Cassian, Gregory the Great, Pseudo-Dionysius, Maximus Confessor, St. Bernard, Hugh of St. Victor, Thomas Aquinas, etc."[21] Even for Thomas Aquinas, who had more respect for bodily life than most, the sense of bodily touch is fraught with danger because Aquinas believed it never participated in reason.[22] So, too, philosophers such as Plato, Descartes, and Kant rejected the body and the emotions as sources of wisdom.

Divorcing the body from human reason does not do justice to the reality of human embodiment. In *Erotic Morality: The Role of Touch in Moral Agency*, religious ethicist Linda Holler discusses scientific studies that show that lack of tactile sensations and deprivation of touch alter brain chemistry and disable our capacities for both cognitive development and the experience of connections to ourselves, others, and the more-than-human-world. Deprivation of touch in constricted emotional environments, including patriarchal, class elitist, and racist environments severely damages people's intellectual abilities and moral compass. Sensory/emotional deprivation disconnects people from their bodies and their awareness of being interdependent on others, including on the abused and increasingly fragile body of our mother, the earth. Such alienation gives rise to violent touch associated with sexual abuse and other forms of violence, such as poverty and war. These are experiences that result in sensory and emotional numbness. Such trauma alters brain chemistry and the moral ability to have just relations with ourselves and others.

Because "cognition emerges in the totality of the lived body" and is grounded "in our sensory-emotional life," Holler proposes that psychological studies of major Western thinkers reveal their affinities with those who suffer from autism, that is, not being able to tolerate sensory experience, and with schizophrenia, being disconnected from the body and overwhelmed by thought processes.[23] Therefore, such people—and here I would include major Western philosophers and theologians—are limited guides to social reality. Until we are fully in touch with and respectful of the material world, we are likely not to know the embodied meaning and consequences of our actions. What Holler cites as "the philosopher's disease" is surely also the theologian's disease.[24]

Given human interdependence with one another and the earth, compassion is a form of emotional intelligence. Given this radical interdependence, compassion for others is also a form of self-love and self-survival. When we are not in touch physically and emotionally with ourselves and others, we lack the critical awareness necessary for moral action. Consequently, when the emotional life is less than healthy, there is little that ethical prescriptions and theological dogma alone can do, *for moral wisdom and insight emanate primarily from sensuous relationships, not precepts.* Therefore, people who live in avoidance and denial of dimensions of their own embodiment neither participate in self-love nor make very loving neighbors. As Perkinson says, white culture and white theology must "grow up spiritually" and "leave the innocence of the suburbs" and embrace the fact that bodies are vulnerable and "that tragedy is irreducible and death is real."[25] Until whites can "groan" and embrace their own reality, they will not be able to "plunge into the depths of the world" as Jesus did when he entered the experience of those "whose bodies were under assault."[26] Fear of needy bodies, Perkinson argues, cannot be assuaged by racist projection; ease requires "organizing a new identity" as white people.[27] In direct contrast to much of the dominant academic philosophical and theological traditions, a call to create new identities as whites necessitates new ethics, new dogma, and new social and institutional practices that embody sensuous connections with ourselves and others. This is the only basis for authentic moral knowing and moral action regarding anti-racist struggle and planetary survival. Toward this end, theologians must recover more fully the mandate of self-love and solidarity in Christian tradition.

Insofar as they resisted white supremacy and managed to love themselves, diverse communities of color have not been as self-alienated as many white people. As sociologist Becky Thompson shows in her study of white activism, at every stage of the white anti-racist struggle in the past four decades, white people's accomplishments were due to the leadership and mentoring of people of color. The instructive modeling of communities of color guided white people's most effective work.[28]

White people must continue to explore the profound losses from racism, starting with the destruction of communities, cultures, and the dreams of people of color, both past and present. Whites must also uncover the destruction that white racism has done to them and the profound need they have to understand salvation differently. I would insist that this is the particular responsibility of the white theological community charged with the work of connecting the values in theological traditions to concrete social realities.

The lesson here is that transforming economic and erotic relations for everyone, including whites, is foundational to the struggle against racism and, indeed, to the survival of a viable future for all. With regard to economic disempowerment, capitalist racism erodes social solidarity and divides the majority working class, which in U.S. history has had more whites than people of color.

With regard to erotic disempowerment, capitalist racism repudiates and disallows what Argentinean theologian Marcella Althaus-Reid calls "the excessiveness of our hungry lives: our hunger for food . . . for the touch of other bodies, for love and for God: a multitude of hungers never satisfied."[29] Because white culture and white theology and the traditions we have been given must be challenged to the core, white theologians and ethicists have our work cut out for us. Any theology that is dualistic and supports the need for certainty, any theology that supports hierarchy, and any theology that is anti-body and erotophobic, is racist. James Perkinson argues that any theology "that locates identity and wholeness entirely on one side of a [binary structure of] opposition" is racist.[30] Christian ethicist Traci West agrees when she writes that God's "power and mystery [are] multiply located and shared" so that theological claims and moral knowledge are racist unless they are generated "from diverse traditions and places," especially in the particularities of victim-survivors of abuse.[31] We all must shoulder the responsibility to reformulate theory, knowledge, and practice to confront the existing theological impoverishment and disorder by connecting religious traditions to concrete social realities. As we keep on in this struggle, remember the wisdom of poet W. H. Auden, who rightly remarked, "As a rule, it is the pleasure-haters who become unjust."[32]

Notes

[1] For an exploration of the tip of the iceberg of white racial overprivilege, see Mary Elizabeth Hobgood, *Dismantling Privilege: An Ethics of Accountability* (Cleveland, OH: Pilgrim Press, 2000), 36–62.

[2] A few of the many scholars of color who have contributed to this expanding literature include bell hooks, Audre Lorde, Patricia Hill Collins, Patricia Williams, Barbara Smith, Gloria Anzaldua, Cherrie Moraga, Carla Trujillo, Lisa C. Ikemoto, Elaine H. Kim, Paula Gun Allen, Himani Bannerji, and Sunera Thobani. White women scholars working on white privilege include Lillian Smith, Peggy McIntosh, Ruth Frankenberg, Minnie Bruce Pratt, Stephanie M. Wildman, Elizabeth Spelman, and Barbara Andolsen.

[3] Linda Holler, *Erotic Morality: The Role of Touch in Moral Agency* (New Brunswick, NJ: Rutgers University Press, 2002), 171.

[4] Quoted in Becky Thompson, "Time Travelling and Border Crossing: Reflections on White Identity," in *Names We Call Home: Autobiography on Racial Identity*, ed. Becky Thompson and Sangeeta Tagi (New York: Routledge, 1996), 103.

[5] See, for example, Dolores Williams, "Black Woman's Surrogacy Experience and the Christian Notion of Redemption," in *After Patriarchy: Feminist Transformations of the World Religions*, ed. Paula M. Cooey, William R. Eakin, and Jay B. McDaniel (Maryknoll, NY: Orbis Books, 1991); Jacquelyn Grant, "The Sin of Servanthood," in *A Troubling in My Soul: Womanist Perspectives on Evil and Suffering*, ed. Emilie M. Townes (Maryknoll, NY: Orbis Books, 1993), 199–218.

[6] Ian F. Haney Lopez, "White by Law," in *Critical Race Theory: The Cutting Edge*, ed. Richard DelGado (Philadelphia: Temple University Press, 1995), 548.

[7] For a myriad of examples, see David R. Roediger, ed., *Black on White: Black Writers on What It Means to Be White* (New York: Schocken Books, 1998).

[8] Bryan N. Massingale, "James Cone and Recent Episcopal Teaching on Racism," *Theological Studies* 61, no. 4 (December 2000): 729.

[9] Ibid.

[10] Eric Williams, *Capitalism and Slavery* (Chapel Hill: University of North Carolina Press, 1944, 1994).

[11] Theodore Allen, *The Invention of the White Race* (New York: Verso, 1997), 244.

[12] Ibid., 211.

[13] Michael Zweig, *The Working Class Majority: America's Best Kept Secret* (Ithaca, NY: Cornell University Press, 2000), 16–19.

[14] Ibid., 30–31.

[15] Ibid., 89.

[16] Doug Henwood, cited in ibid., 32.

[17] Thomas C. Holt, "The Essence of the Contract: The Articulation of Race, Gender, and Political Economy in British Emancipation Policy, 1838–1866," in *Beyond Slavery: Exploration of Race, Labor and Citizenship in Postemancipation Societies*, ed. Frederick Cooper, Thomas C. Holt, and Rebecca J. Scott (Chapel Hill: University of North Carolina Press, 2000), 33–59.

[18] M. Shawn Copeland, "Guest Editorial," *Theological Studies* 61, no. 4 (December 2000): 604.

[19] James W. Perkinson, *White Theology: Outing Supremacy in Modernity* (New York: Palgrave Macmillan, 2004), 189.

[20] Ibid., 75.

[21] J. Giles Milhaven, "A Medieval Lesson in Bodily Knowing," *AAR Journal of the American Academy of Religion* 62, no. 2 (September 1989): 353.

[22] Ibid., 359.

[23] Holler, *Erotic Morality*, 60–61, 15, 81.

[24] Ibid., 60, 79–81, 84–88, 114.

[25] Perkinson, *White Theology*, 199, 202.

[26] Ibid., 244, 247.

[27] Ibid., 167.

[28] Becky Thompson, *A Promise and a Way of Life: White Anti-Racist Activism* (Minneapolis: University of Minnesota Press, 2001).

[29] Marcella Althaus-Reid, *Indecent Theology: Perversions in Sex, Gender and Politics* (New York: Routledge, 2000), 200.

[30] Perkinson, *White Theology*, 245.

[31] Traci C. West, *Disruptive Christian Ethics: When Racism and Women's Lives Matter* (Louisville, KY: Westminster John Knox Press, 2006), esp. 69, 113.

[32] W. H. Auden, quoted in Virginia Ramey Mollenkott, *Sensuous Spirituality: Out from Fundamentalism* (New York: Crossroad Publications, 1993), 158.

3

• • • •

SOCIAL JUSTICE, THE COMMON GOOD, AND NEW SIGNS OF RACISM

Barbara Hilkert Andolsen

American Catholic social ethicists as a group have failed consistently to probe racism as a major problem in our national life. This failure on the part of Catholic social ethicists is only one piece of a larger failure by the American Roman Catholic Church and the United States as a national community to struggle in a persistent way to redress longstanding and dire racial inequalities in our common life. Lack of attention to racial injustices has serious import for the comprehensiveness and adequacy of contemporary American Catholic social thought. Moral theologian Bryan N. Massingale has warned clearly that a "Catholic failure to engage adequately the pivotal issue of racial injustice would decisively compromise its theology of justice."[1] This essay stresses the importance of a constantly updated understanding of racial injustices in order to advocate wisely for the moral values of social justice and the common good in American national life.

It is imperative for American Catholic moral theologians to be constantly attentive to the differences, positive and negative, that race makes in our individual and collective lives. Some readers of this essay will be concerned that I appear to essentialize race. That is contrary to my intention. Race is sometimes understood as a system for grouping human beings into subgroups based upon constellations of inherited physiological features, including skin hue, hair texture, and a range of facial features and body types. Such understandings of race are vigorously disputed by geneticists, biologists, and social scientists. The history of changing ideas about race shows that race is a socially constructed category. This essay is consistent with the view that race *as a socially constructed reality* often continues to have *powerful* effects on the life plans and experiences of individuals and on the operation and maintenance of key social institutions. Moreover, the impact of race is not morally neutral because it remains deeply intertwined with the injustices that followed in the wake of European colonialism and American imperialism.

At present, whiteness as a racial category is socially constructed in ways that carry manifold social advantages. The social construction of blackness—in which whites are actively involved, either to maintain the status quo or to contribute to its transformation—is weighed down by many social burdens. Differences between Native Americans and others in this nation reveal a tragic history as well. Asian immigrants and their descendants and people of Hawaiian or Pacific origin have faced and continue to face specific forms of dispossession and discrimination. While ethnic groups such as Mexican Americans or Puerto Ricans (categorized by the Census Bureau under the general term Hispanic or Latino) are not officially designated as racial groups, they face discrimination similar to racial discrimination.

American Catholic social ethicists need to seek out discussions and written sources in which those from various racial/ethnic groups describe and analyze their experiences and share their visions of a flourishing human life. White ethicists need to listen to and to be accountable to persons from other racial groups. We need to interrogate our white experiences to recognize and to change demeaning racial attitudes and beliefs and to understand and resist participation in racially unjust social structures. However, a comprehensive examination of racial and ethnic differences as these play out in multiple forms of social injustice is far beyond the scope of this short essay. While I want to acknowledge that race is not a simple social binary, for purposes of this essay I concentrate on white and black social experiences in patterns of residency and in employment.

Promoting justice begins with a serious effort to discern the key contours of current social life. Is there evidence that some people are deprived of the minimal resources necessary for dignified life

in the community? Are there indications that some people or
groups of people have been relegated to the fringes of society,
unable to participate in a reasonably satisfying way in the life of
the community? Do social institutions function to marginalize
certain groups while maintaining a pattern of excessive social
privileges for another group or groups? The concept of social
justice prods us to ask such questions about society's treatment
of persons and about the fairness of the outcomes produced by
interlocking social institutions. Justice spurs us to examine who
gets what share of important social goods, such as education,
employment, and social respect. Justice also presses us to ask
who has which opportunities for participation in important social activities and decision making. As the U.S. Catholic bishops
tell us, "social justice implies that persons have an obligation to
be active and productive participants in the life of society and
that society has a duty to enable them to participate in this way."[2]
This essay examines some ways in which race distorts opportunities to be active participants in neighborhood life or in the work-
place.

Since the civil rights movement of the 1950s and 1960s, there
has been real progress in many aspects of race relations in the
United States. The Civil Rights Act of 1964 legally prohibited
discrimination in employment, education, voting, and public ac-
commodations based on race, color, or ethnic origin. Segregation
practices in public facilities—from separate water fountains to
separate schools—were ended. Minority voting rights have been
safeguarded, and this has led to the election of more African
American political leaders. The black middle class experienced a
large expansion during the second half of the twentieth century.
All this social progress should be acknowledged and celebrated.
However, there are many remaining social symptoms that suggest that white racism and its sequelae continue to scar our national life. What the U.S. Catholic bishops said more than twenty-
five years ago in *Brothers and Sisters to Us* remains disappointingly
accurate today:

> Crude and blatant expressions of racist sentiment, though
> they occasionally exist, are today considered bad form. Yet
> racism itself persists in covert ways. Under the guise of other
> motives, it is manifest in the tendency to stereotype and

> marginalize whole segments of the population whose pres-
> ence is perceived as a threat. It is manifest also in the indif-
> ference that replaces open hatred. The minority poor are
> seen as the dross of a post-industrial society—without skills,
> without motivation, without incentive. They are expend-
> able.[3]

Far too many African Americans are marginalized in society in
multiple ways that violate the norm of justice as participation.

Following the lead of Catholic ethicist David Hollenbach, this
essay also explores how far short American society has fallen in
its quest to promote the "good of the people understood inclu-
sively."[4] Hollenbach insists that the reality that so many African
Americans are trapped in socially isolated pockets of urban poverty is a crucial sign that this society has failed to achieve the
common good. Hollenbach's analysis of the current social and
economic situation—relying on the work of certain black sociologists, especially Orlando Patterson and William Julius Wil-
son—emphasizes the importance of social class over race in cir-
cumscribing the life chances of poor blacks. He writes: "Racial
prejudice is no longer the principal cause of urban poverty in the
United States today. Thus greater racial tolerance will not provide the principal solution."[5] Hollenbach acknowledges that racism remains a serious social evil. However, in his discussion of
racism he seems to focus on overt beliefs about or feelings of
white racial superiority. The solution to such racism, as he under-
stands it, is a racial tolerance that respects individuals without
regard for color or race. In this essay I rely on an understanding
of white racism that emphasizes more strongly the unjust impact
of social practices, structures, and institutions that consistently
result in disproportionate social benefits for whites and social
burdens for blacks. My reading of the social situation seeks to
maintain a focus on the complex interconnections *between race
and social class* in American society. While I stress race and racism more than Hollenbach does, his work is very important because of the way in which he has used the norm of the common
good to illuminate vividly the moral issue created by the social
abandonment of poor African Americans in urban ghettos.

The centrality of the common good as a norm is an important
strength in Roman Catholic moral theology. The common good

refers to the moral quality of communal life. The good society is one organized in a fashion conducive to the human flourishing of *each and every* member of the community. We citizens collectively are accountable to those with whom we find ourselves in civic relationships—broadly defined. As sharers in a joint civic life, the members of a society are mutually accountable for maintaining a morally decent life together. Racial differences do not negate or minimize shared obligations to strive for a positive quality of common life. When racist social structures seriously constrict the life opportunities of far too many African Americans, there are disturbing shortcomings in achieving a common good for American society. During a United Nations' conference on racism and xenophobia in 2001, a Vatican representative warned: "Too often in history, uncritical societies have stood by inactive as *new signs of racism* raised their head. If we are not alert, hatred and racial intolerance can reappear in any society, no matter how advanced it may consider itself" (emphasis added).[6] The national failure in the United States to grapple more successfully with shifting and, hence, "new" signs of racial inequality in our common life results in a serious, ongoing diminution of justice and of the common good in our national life.

Hurricane Katrina and Racial Perceptions

The life-threatening consequences of our failures to address deeply intertwined issues of race and economic class constructively played out to the nation's (short-lived) horror on television screens in late August and early September 2005, when Hurricane Katrina struck New Orleans. In the immediate aftermath of the storm vital levees were breached, flooding 80 percent of the land in this majority black city. Vast numbers of mainly poor, black residents who lacked the resources to heed evacuation calls were stranded for days as local, state, and national officials struggled ineptly to rescue them.

A disturbing poll conducted right after these events by the Pew Research Center for People and the Press indicated that the flurry of attention paid to race by some media commentators in the immediate aftermath of the hurricane was not likely to lead to greater insights concerning race or deepened commitment to racial justice in the white community. There were serious differences in how whites and blacks perceived the difficulties experienced by those stranded by the flood waters in New Orleans. The Pew survey indicated that only 17 percent of whites felt the federal government's response would have been quicker had "most victims been white," while 66 percent of blacks believed that white victims would have gotten help more quickly. Even more disturbing was the racial disparity in the answers to another of the survey's questions. Seventy-one percent of blacks said the response to Hurricane Katrina demonstrated that "racial inequality remains a major problem." In the immediate aftermath of Katrina, a majority of white Americans—56 percent—did not agree with the statement that the hurricane and its aftermath revealed that racial inequality remains a major social issue. Another 12 percent of whites answered that they did not know whether "racial inequality [was] still a major problem." Thus, immediately after Hurricane Katrina, slightly less than one in three white Americans held the opinion that racial inequality had again been shown to be a major social problem in this country.[7] Among white Catholics a slight majority (51 percent) answered "no" to the question about whether racial inequalities were still a major issue; 10 percent answered "do not know"; and only 39 percent recognized racial inequalities as a major issue.[8]

Thus, even a dramatic event, such as Hurricane Katrina in 2005, fails to provoke most white people to reexamine carefully the terrible consequences of racism in social, political, and economic life in the United States today. However, the centrality of social justice and the common good in Roman Catholic moral theology ought to prompt Catholic social ethicists to give greater priority to the task of consistently updating our understanding of the changing social dynamics of race in this country.

Social Science Information about Racial Injustices

In the remainder of this short essay I share some of the findings from social scientists—economists and sociologists—on two issues that are among the key elements in the current pattern of serious racial inequality in the United States. The two patterns that I discuss are the concentration of poor African American groups in declining inner-city neighborhoods, particularly in the Northeast and Midwest. The other is a review of evidence that many African Americans continue to confront unjust employment barriers in the U.S. economy. These are not the only important issues where we can learn much from following developments carefully in the social-science literature. Two other topics that surely are of crucial importance to understand contemporary racial injustices are educational patterns for African Americans and persistent inequalities in health care, both in access to health care and in outcomes. However, in this short essay I have chosen to focus on housing and jobs.

Residential Segregation

In a *Washington Post* op-ed piece in the immediate aftermath of Hurricane Katrina, Eugene Robinson said, "It's as if we don't even see poor people in this country anymore, as if we don't even try to imagine what their lives are like."[9] One of the reasons many white Americans "don't see" poor black Americans is an insufficiently acknowledged pattern of segregation of poor blacks in inner-city neighborhoods that many whites rarely visit. The problem of residential segregation in metropolitan areas is crucial for African Americans because more than 85 percent of the African American population of the United States in 2000 lived in urban areas.[10]

The concentration of African Americans predominantly in discrete urban neighborhoods is a phenomenon that Douglas S. Massey and Nancy A. Denton provocatively described in 1993 as American apartheid. In the book with that title these scholars declared that "our research indicates that racial residential segregation is the principal structural feature of American society responsible for the perpetuation of urban poverty." They go on to say that residential segregation "represents a primary cause of racial inequality in the United States."[11] In the later half of the twentieth century, as many whites left the central cities for the suburbs, African Americans, especially lower-income African Americans, were left behind in neighborhoods that became "progressively isolated—geographically, socially, and economically—from the rest of society."[12]

Massey's and Denton's important book analyzed the situation through the early 1990s. There has been some modest improvement according to the 2000 census, in patterns of residential segregation. Indeed, a slow trend toward greater racial integration in residential patterns has been apparent since the 1970s. Disappointingly, the rate of decline in residential segregation was less over the 1990s than it had been over the 1980s.

Problems of residential segregation among racial groups remain severe in many major cities in the United States. African Americans continue to face more residential separation than any other minority group. Residential segregation by race remains pronounced, particularly in the Northeast. The problem is less severe in the Old South where, despite even historical "Jim Crow" segregation, whites and blacks have a long history of living in residential proximity. Still, some recent data shows an increase in residential segregation in some major Southern cities.[13] Residential segregation is also less prevalent in the Southwest and Northwest, perhaps because African Americans are a smaller part of the population in those areas. In fact, the demographic movement of blacks into integrated neighborhoods in cities that have a small but growing black population is a key factor in the slow decline of residential segregation throughout the United States.[14] When sociologists report a modest trend toward blacks living in more diverse neighborhoods, it is more likely to be a neighborhood with Hispanics or Asian Americans than it is to be a neighborhood with whites. According to John Logan and his colleagues, "Whites were the most racially isolated of the groups from 1980 to 2000," although their isolation from other groups did decline during that period.[15]

Some might respond that African Americans' congregating in homogeneous urban neighborhoods is not necessarily a disturbing trend. Such people might be recalling positive family memories of the Polish or Italian neighborhoods where their great-grandparents settled when they first came to this country. However, comparing inner-city black neighborhoods with immigrant neighborhoods past and present, Massey and Denton insist that

> No group in the history of the United States has ever experienced the sustained high level of residential segregation that has been imposed on blacks in large American cities for the past 50 years. This extreme racial isolation did not just happen; it was manufactured by whites through a series of

self-conscious actions and purposeful institutional arrangements that continue today.[16]

One example of an institutional practice that serves to bolster residential segregation is unequal treatment of similarly situated mortgage applicants from different racial groups. A major study analyzing 2004 home-loan data has shown that mortgage lenders are more likely to offer minority home loan applicants mortgage financing on less favorable terms—so-called sub-prime mortgages. Minority group applicants with similar credit scores and comparable down payments were more likely to be offered sub-prime loans than were similar white applicants. Sub-prime financing involves higher interest rates and higher borrowing costs, so minority clients pushed toward these unfavorable loans can only afford to own less valuable houses in less desirable neighborhoods.[17]

The moral difficulty posed by these institutionally perpetuated patterns of residential segregation is stated eloquently by law professor Charles R. Lawrence, who was discussing the closely related phenomenon of school segregation. He declared: "The genius of segregation as a tool of oppression is in the signal it sends to the oppressors—that their monopoly on resources is legitimate, that there is no need for sharing, no moral requirement of empathy and care."[18] Given the pervasive, albeit slowly declining reality of residential segregation in the United States, whites—including white Catholics—find that blacks are literally not their neighbors (nor their fellow parishioners in a system of neighborhood parishes).

Race and Employment

Another crucial issue at the intersection of race and class is the changing nature of jobs in the United States, with the increasing polarization of rewards from work. In 1979 the American Catholic bishops said presciently in *Brothers and Sisters to Us*:

> We wish to call attention to the persistent presence of racism and in particular to the relationship between racial and economic justice. Racism and economic oppression are distinct but interrelated forces which dehumanize our society.

. . . Our economic structures are undergoing fundamental changes which threaten to intensify social inequalities in our nation. We are entering an era characterized by limited resources, restricted job markets and dwindling revenues. In this atmosphere, the poor and racial minorities are being asked to bear the heaviest burden of the new economic pressures.[19]

Those heavier economic burdens that are still being borne by the African American community include both a persistently higher rate of unemployment and a more devastating impact from the loss of good manufacturing jobs.

While there is some limited good news about declines in residential segregation by race in the decade of the 1990s, there has been continuing disturbing information about black employment. During the 1990s employment rates for young, less educated "black men aged 16 through 24 . . . actually dropped. In fact, this group's employment declined more during the 1990s (when it fell from 59 percent to 52 percent) than during the preceding decade (when it fell from 62 percent to 59 percent)."[20] In addition to declining employment rates there has been a declining rate of labor-force participation. This means that too many younger black men are not even looking for work. One reason that black men are probably discouraged about looking for work is the disappearance of many relatively well-paying manufacturing jobs.

Greater difficulty in employment for African Americans is a pattern that has continued into the new millennium. In the early twenty-first century the United States has experienced an economic expansion that has been unusually anemic when it comes to job creation or economic payoffs for ordinary workers. The bursting of the dot-com bubble at the beginning of the twenty-first century and the accompanying decline in the American labor market were particularly hard on blacks—and not just blacks with lesser education. In 2003 an article in *Business Week* reported:

Since the stock market bubble burst in March 2000, black unemployment has soared to nearly 11%, double that of whites. And it's not just less skilled blacks who got hurt. In

2002, the number of employed black managers and professionals fell. . . . Meanwhile, the number of employed white managers and professionals continued to rise.[21]

While whites saw employment recover at a tepid pace after the recession of 2001, African Americans were still losing jobs as late as 2005. While this was true for African American women, the major factor in the negative black unemployment picture in 2005 was significantly increased African American male unemployment.[22] Continuing high black unemployment during a period of economic recovery is especially worrisome because black unemployment is more cyclically sensitive than white unemployment. Blacks are more likely to lose jobs during a recession. But, in the late twentieth century, blacks also benefited in terms of employment during expansionary periods. White employment had shown a less cyclical swing.[23] Thus, it is a real cause for concern that black unemployment continued to decline as the economy improved from 2001 to 2005.

There is social-science evidence that continuing discrimination against job applicants on the basis of race plays a role in black people's current employment difficulties. In one experiment conducted in 2001 and 2002, Marianne Bertrand and Sendhil Mullainathan tested reactions to resumes sent in response to help-wanted ads placed by employers in Boston and Chicago. During the course of the study the authors submitted five thousand resumes for thirteen hundred advertised positions. Some resumes had names associated with whites, such as Emily Walsh or Greg Baker. Other matching resumes had names that sounded black, such as Lakisha Washington or Jamal Jones. Holding all else equal, the "white" applicants were 50 percent more likely to be invited for a job interview. Some fictitious resumes for each group had superior credentials. "White" applicants with superior credentials got more favorable responses than their "black" counterparts. Thus, even well-qualified "black" applicants were less likely to be invited for a job interview than their "white" peers.[24]

In this study there was also evidence of a troubling connection between residential segregation by race and job opportunities. The investigators systematically varied the addresses on resumes. They reported, "We find that living in a wealthier (or more educated or Whiter) neighborhood increases call back rates."[25] The study's authors conclude "differential treatment by race still appears to . . . be prominent in the U.S. labor market."[26]

A number of social-science scholars would add that less-educated black men in particular are having more difficulty finding jobs in an economy where an increasing proportion of jobs are service jobs, not manufacturing jobs. There is evidence that a number of employers hold unfavorable perceptions of some African American job applicants. While these perceptions present difficulties for African American women, the most unfavorable perceptions concern African American men with less education. Philip Moss and Chris Tilly investigated this problem in a study for the Sage Foundation. The study focused on applicants for jobs that require, at most, a high school education. The researchers relied on interviews with human-resource decision makers in Atlanta, Boston, Detroit, and Los Angeles. Despite strong social pressures against admitting racial prejudice, a surprising number of interviewees divulged negative perceptions about what Moss and Tilly called the "soft skills" of black inner-city applicants— particularly black male applicants. These authors "define *soft skills* as skills, abilities, and traits that pertain to personality, attitude, and behavior rather than to formal or technical knowledge."[27] The project leaders admit that, when analyzing the responses collected, it was sometimes difficult to differentiate between accurate perceptions of variations in human relationship skills (such as customer-service skills) and racial stereotypes. They concede that "prejudice and rational economic decision making are tangled together in employers' perceptions."[28] Later, they rephrase this point interestingly when they state that "U.S. employers typically state prejudicial views of racial and ethnic groups *in terms of skill*; they speak the language of 'modern' or 'laissez-faire' racism, making it difficult to distinguish prejudice from accurate perceptions of skill differences."[29]

Moss and Tilly found managerial perceptions that blacks were overly sensitive to criticism about work performance or hostile in their interaction with co-workers, supervisors, or customers. A human-resource manager for a public-sector employer in Los Angeles said, for example: "A lot of these young black men who are being tough scare some of their supervisors. And so rather than address their behavior problems and deal with the issues, they will back away until they can find a way to get rid of them."

She concluded, "We have a tendency to fear what we're not real familiar with."[30]

Moss and Tilly also found connections between residential segregation and economic disadvantage. In their interviews, negative perceptions about the skills and work attitudes of less educated black applicants were compounded by the negative perceptions that some employers had about applicants living in inner-city neighborhoods. "This composite [negative] image works to the detriment of inner-city workers of color."[31] For example, Moss and Tilly reminded their readers that many prospective employers actively recruit employees, often striving to attract workers from preferred groups. A number of employers interviewed for this study said they only placed job advertisements in suburban newspapers, because they viewed suburban applicants as better qualified.

Moss and Tilly were even uneasy about the absence of comments about inner-city workers in some interviews with suburban employers. The two researchers report that "many suburban employers don't concern themselves *at all* with the inner city. They don't have employees from the inner city, they do not consider recruiting there, and they do not even remotely consider locating there. . . . the inner city has been erased as a possibility, either purposefully or because of distance."[32] It is difficult—both because of transportation difficulties and commuting times and because of negative employer perceptions—for inner-city applicants to get jobs in the suburbs. It is also less likely that employers from outside the center city will create new jobs in downtown locations. So inner-city blacks are all but locked out of the employment opportunities suburban customers and businesses are generating.

Black Female Workers Lose Ground

Labor-market equality continues to be an important issue for black women, too. As a feminist scholar, I am particularly concerned that the economic fortunes of whites and black women working full time have continued to diverge for almost the last quarter-century. In the immediate wake of the civil rights movement and the second wave of feminism (in the 1960s and 1970s), the earnings gap between white female and black female workers began to close, reaching parity by 1979. However, the gap *re-opened* in the 1980s. A recent analysis by Irene Browne and Rachel Askew shows that the breach between white and black women "remained fairly constant—neither widening nor closing" in the 1990s or early 2000s.[33] It is particularly disturbing to see that this persistent gap occurs at about the same level for black women who have a college education as it does for their counterparts who failed to complete high school. "Among both high school dropouts and college graduates, the Black-White earnings differential decreased slightly in the early 1990s and then increased somewhat in the later half of the decade and into the 21st century."[34] Brown and Askew emphasize the point that I believe has even broader applications than the specifics of their study. These two researchers say: "Our study has demonstrated the dynamic nature of labor market inequality. Wage parity of one point in time does not imply that racial/ethnic inequality among women has ended."[35]

Racial Progress, Justice, and the Common Good

The fact that progress in earnings equality between white and black women could be eroded is a point that Catholic social ethicists need to take seriously. There have been important gains in racial justice since the civil rights movement of the 1960s. However, there is no inevitable social dynamic that guarantees only forward movement toward greater racial justice. Social gains—such as the virtual wage parity between black and white women in the late 1970s—can be undermined. Social ethicists need to heed the Vatican's caution that new signs of racism can emerge in societies that pride themselves on having made racial progress.

This essay is pressing the point that in many areas of American life racial inequalities continue to shift their contours. Therefore, Roman Catholic moral theologians need to be in persistent dialogue with social scientists to understand the specific parameters of racial inequality in contemporary society. I am arguing that carrying on *sustained* conversations among Roman Catholic ethicists about race is also crucial in order for us to do adequate work in moral theology here in the United States.

The norm of social justice prods us to take action to bring about social transformation when existing social patterns, such as patterns of residential segregation and employment practices, leave certain socially vulnerable racial groups consistently marginalized in social life.

In a U.S. context one cannot challenge racial marginalization as a violation of social justice without having a clear understanding of the contemporary ways in which racial patterns in areas such as housing or employment leave many African Americans at the margins of society. Massey and Denton have turned our attention to poor black neighborhoods throughout America that have become "progressively isolated—geographically, socially, and economically—from the rest of society."[36] When disproportionately large numbers of African Americans are unemployed or out of the labor force completely, serious questions about justice as participation are raised.

Moreover, there cannot be a genuine common good in the United States unless longstanding, but evolving, patterns of racial injustice are constructively addressed. White Americans share a moral responsibility for the ethical caliber of communal life in the United States—a national life (with all its racial injustices) that was a work in progress when we "joined" the community. There are historical, cultural, economic, and social bonds that join racial and ethnic groups in the United States. Those civic bonds were not—and are not—always positive ones. The moral ideal of the common good challenges us to work toward new patterns of just relationships that transform those complex intertwined racial and ethnic bonds into life-enhancing, communal ties.

Continuing racial residential segregation is a major threat to the common good, because we literally do not live our lives in common places. Enduring racial disparities in employment means that neither do we work side by side, day in and day out. In the United States many whites can abandon poor blacks to joblessness, bad schools, and social threats such as higher crime rates and greater environmental pollution without being threatened by the same social difficulties themselves. The dire conditions faced by urban ghetto residents do not appear on the surface to threaten comfortable, white, middle-class, suburban lives. Racial segregation in the work place and in our neighborhoods allows whites too rarely to see how far short we have fallen of achieving the common good.

The bishops of England and Wales could have been speaking to U.S. Catholics when they insisted: "The first duty of the citizen towards the common good is to ensure that nobody is marginalised . . . and to bring back into a place in the community those who have been marginalised in the past. The alternative is the creation of an alienated 'underclass', bereft of any sense of participation in or belonging to the wider community."[37] Hurricane Katrina temporarily shocked many white Americans because it exposed a large group of sick and poor people who were denied a basic governmental protection—rescue services in the face of natural disaster. The controversy that ensued about the use of the word *refugees* to describe displaced New Orleanians was significant because it exposed a neuralgic point about who truly belongs as a full member of the community in New Orleans, in Louisiana, and in the United States of America.[38]

In a thoughtful essay on Hurricane Katrina, philosopher Iris Marion Young talked about how difficult it is to struggle with "the paradox that normal practices within which people act with good intentions continue to produce significant evil."[39] She mentioned, in particular, housing patterns that trapped black residents in some of the most flood-prone areas of the city. Another part of the paradox was labor-market patterns in New Orleans that left too many residents without an economic safety line that would have enabled them to leave the city before Katrina hit.

At the end of their research investigating the interlocking factors in gender, race, and class as these contributed to the suffering in the wake of Hurricane Katrina, a group of feminist social scientists asked what level of social inequality "we are willing to tolerate while still laying claim to the ideals of a good and just society."[40] This question about social morality exposes the basic reason why Roman Catholic moral theologians need more diligently to carry on a continuing dialogue about race with such social scientists. Understanding the ways in which racial inequalities diminish the life chances of far too many of our fellow citizens is critical to seeing how much change a commitment to the common good demands from white Americans. According to the *Catechism of the Catholic Church*, "the participation of all in realizing the common good calls for a continually renewed conversion of the social partners."[41] A continually renewed conversion requires that white Catholics in the United States strive continually to update our understanding of the changing dynamics of racial injustice, so that we can more effectively supports actions and policies that promote social justice and the common good in this nation.

Notes

[1] Bryan N. Massingale, "James Cone and Recent Catholic Episcopal Teaching on Racism," *Theological Studies* 61 (2000): 701.

[2] National Conference of Catholic Bishops, *Economic Justice for All: Pastoral Letter on Catholic Social Teaching and the U.S. Economy* (Washington, DC: United States Catholic Conference, 1986), §71.

[3] National Conference of Catholic Bishops, *Brothers and Sisters to Us: U.S. Bishops' Pastoral Letter on Racism in Our Day* (Washington, DC: United States Catholic Conference, 1979). Available at http://www.nccbuscc.org/saac/bishopspastoral.shtml (accessed May 30, 2006).

[4] David Hollenbach, SJ, *The Common Good and Christian Ethics* (New York: Cambridge Press, 2002), 69.

[5] Ibid., 174.

[6] "Intervention by the Head of the Holy See Delegation at the United Nations Organization on Racism, Racial Discrimination, Xenophobia and Related Intolerance," January 28, 2002. Available at http://www.vatican.va (accessed May 30, 2006). Emphasis added.

[7] Pew Research Center for the People and the Press, "Huge Racial Divide over Katrina and Its Consequences," 2. Available at http://people-press.org/reports/pdf/255.pdf (accessed March 17, 2006).

[8] Ibid., 14. The Pew Research Center did not provide statistics on black Catholics in this study.

[9] Eugene Robinson, "No Longer Invisible," *Washington Post*, September 9, 2005, A25.

[10] John Iceland, Daniel Weinberg, and Erika Steinmetz, *Racial and Ethnic Residential Segregation in the United States 1980–2000*, U.S. Census Bureau, Series CENSR-3 (Washington, DC: U.S. Printing Bureau 2002), 59.

[11] Douglas S. Massey and Nancy A. Denton, *American Apartheid: Segregation and the Making of the Underclass* (Cambridge: Harvard University Press, 1993), viii.

[12] Ibid., 2.

[13] Rima Wilkes and John Iceland, "Hypersegregation in the Twenty-first Century," *Demography* 41 (February 2004): 23–36.

[14] John R. Logan, Brian J. Stults, and Reynolds Farley, "Segregation of Minorities in the Metropolis: Two Decades of Change," *Demography* 41 (February 2004): 1–22.

[15] Ibid., 8.

[16] Massey and Denton, *American Apartheid*, 2.

[17] Erik Eckholm, "Black and Hispanic Home Buyers Pay Higher Interest on Mortgages, Study Finds," *New York Times*, June 1, 2006, A22.

[18] Charles R. Lawrence, "Forbidden Conversations: On Race, Privacy, and Community," *Yale Law Journal* 114 (April 2005): 1377.

[19] National Conference of Catholic Bishops, *Brothers and Sisters to Us*.

[20] Harry J. Holzer and Paul Offner, "The Puzzle of Black Male Unemployment," *Public Interest* (Winter 2004), 74–75.

[21] Roger O. Crockett with Peter Coy, "Progress without Parity: Fewer Are Poor, But Blacks Are No Closer to Economic Equality," *Business Week* (July 14, 2003), 100. Available at Proquest, Research Library (accessed January 30, 2006).

[22] Jared Bernstein with Yulia Fungrad, "Economic Snapshots: The African-Americans in the Current Recovery." Available at http://www.epinet.org (accessed January 30, 2006).

[23] Katherine L. Bradbury, "Rising Tide in the Labor Market: To What Degree Do Expansions Benefit the Disadvantaged?" *New England Economic Review* (May/June 2000), 3–33; Kenneth A. Couch and Robert Fairlie, "Last Hired, First Fired? Black-White Unemployment and the Business Cycle," Working Paper 2005–50 (November 2005). Available at http://repec.org (accessed February 3, 2006).

[24] Marianne Bertrand and Sendhil Mullainathan, "Are Emily and Greg More Employable Than Lakisha and Jamal? A Field Experiment on Labor Market Discrimination," *American Economic Review* 94 (September 2004): 992.

[25] Ibid.

[26] Ibid., 991.

[27] Philip Moss and Chris Tilly, *Stories Employers Tell: Race, Skill, and Hiring in America* (New York: Russell Sage Foundation, 2001), 44.

[28] Ibid., 4.

[29] Ibid., 88–89.

[30] Ibid., 101.

[31] Ibid., 156.

[32] Ibid., 173.

[33] Irene Browne and Rachel Askew, "Race, Ethnicity, and Wage Inequality among Women: What Happened in the 1990s and Early 21st Century?" *American Behavioral Scientist* 48 (May 2005): 1276.

[34] Ibid., 1283.

[35] Ibid., 1287.

[36] Massey and Denton, *American Apartheid*, 2.

[37] Catholic Bishops' Conference of England and Wales, *The Common Good and the Catholic Church's Social Teaching* (1996), §75. Available at http://www.cori.ie/justice/cath_soc_thought/otherdocs/common_good.htm (accessed March 31, 2006).

[38] Robert E. Pierre and Paul Farhi, "'Refugee': A Word of Trouble," *Washington Post*, September 7, 2005, C1. Some people insisted that the word *refugee* is a term limited to persons who flee from violent upheavals or natural disasters in their country to another country where they are not citizens. The controversy about the use of the word *refugee,* therefore, had to do with recognition of displaced people from New Orleans as fellow citizens of these United States.

[39] Iris Young, "Katrina: Too Much Blame, Not Enough Responsibility," *Dissent* 53 (Winter 2006): 42.

[40] Barbara Gault et al., "The Women of New Orleans and the Gulf Coast: Multiple Disadvantages and Key Assets for Recovery, Part I: Poverty, Race, Gender, and Class," Institute for Women's Policy Research Briefing Paper IWPR#D464 (October 2005): 12.

[41] *Catechism of the Catholic Church* (Vatican City: Libreria Editrice), 1.

PART II

THE STRUGGLE TO NAME
WHITE PRIVILEGE

4

• • • •

WHITE PRIVILEGE

My Theological Journey

Charles E. Curran

This essay, an autobiographical narrative reflecting on my awareness of racism and white privilege in my theological journey, has not been easy to write. In the last few years, I have become somewhat educated about racism and white privilege. I have to face the reality that I barely recognized the problem of racism in my own somewhat extensive writings and was blithely unaware of my own white privilege.

Racism

The references to racism in my writings are very few, and there is never any concentrated discussion of the issue. This lack is especially telling in a moral theologian who often dealt with social ethics. Other theologians, because of the focus of their discipline, might not have the same opportunities to discuss and evaluate racism.

In my 1982 monograph *American Catholic Social Ethics: Twentieth Century Approaches* I analyzed and critiqued the writings of

A version of this chapter was presented to the white privilege and racism developing group of the Catholic Theological Society of America, June 2005.

five figures in Catholic social ethics. The index has seven references to race discrimination and racism. The two most extended
discussions (at best, a few pages each) deal with Paul Hanly Furfey
and John A. Ryan. Looking back now on what I wrote then, I am
very embarrassed and uncomfortable.

Paul Hanly Furfey, the Catholic University of America sociologist, in the 1930s, developed a Christian personalist approach
to ethics based on the Catholic Worker model. The radical gospel
ethic strongly criticizes the social ethos in the United States. Personalist action calls for the twofold strategy of separation and
nonparticipation, on the one hand, and bearing witness, on the
other hand. Furfey, in his writings, emphasizes three significant
issues—poverty, racism, and war. He strongly condemns Catholic conformity in all these areas. Furfey, the sociologist, points
out the grave evils in racial segregation and discrimination in all
aspects of life. For Catholics this is a serious moral obligation—
a matter of eternal life or death.[1]

I disagreed with Furfey's approach but praised his recognition
of the three deep problems facing our country—poverty, race,
and war—issues that have remained very important in our society. Catholic liberals tend to overlook these deep problems, "but
the radical possesses a methodological approach which makes
one sensitive to the real problems facing our society."[2] In later
writings I have addressed issues of poverty and peace, but I have
never dealt the same way with racism. I did not follow up on
what I had recognized and written in 1982!

The other comments in this book refer to John A. Ryan, the
premier Catholic social ethicist in the first half of the twentieth
century. In the 1920s Ryan urged his student, Fr. Francis Gilligan,
to write a pioneer doctoral dissertation under his direction entitled *The Morality of the Color Line*.[3] But Ryan himself did not
discuss racism in any depth, and I negatively criticized two of his
comments about racism. With regard to interracial marriages,
Ryan mentioned that the church prudently urges her pastors to
conform to laws banning such marriages, and few if any priests
or bishops have been accused of violating these laws. My reaction was, "His comments on the issue were totally conforming
without a hint of the prophetic."[4]

I described as "disappointing" a lecture he gave in 1943 at Howard University in Washington. After identifying many of the existing problems of racial discrimination, he called for active leadership and the avoidance of violence, urged patience, and recommended working with people of good will in the white community. Ryan's great contribution to social ethics was his insistence on the need for government intervention. But there was no mention of law or government intervention in the area of racism.[5] Thus, I criticized Ryan, but I am open to even deeper negative criticism.

Only in the last few years have I become conscious of my failure to recognize the problems of racism in the United States and in the Catholic church. My friend and would-be student Bryan Massingale correctly pointed out the failure of contemporary Catholic moral theologians, myself included, to deal with the evil of racism.[6]

Massingale has also pointed out two windows of convergence of black theology and racism with Catholic theology—the Catholic recognition of social or structural sin and solidarity with the poor.[7] Margaret Pfeil uses the option for the poor to attack white privilege.[8] I have made many references in my writings to these three aspects but have never connected them with racism beyond an occasional word or phrase. So, despite having the tools that should have made me more aware of the problem of racism, I never really addressed racism in my writings.

I could offer many excuses, but they would be only excuses. Actually, I did pay a little attention to racism in my classes. In the late 1960s I worked on occasion with J. Deotis Roberts, who was then teaching at Howard University. We were involved in one or two projects together, and he graciously accepted one of my students into his classes at Howard. I assigned his book on liberation and reconciliation in my classes on social and political ethics.[9] A few years later I also used my friend Dan Maguire's book *A New American Justice*.[10] I continued my association with Deotis in both the Society of Christian Ethics and the American Theological Society. Three years ago I was invited to contribute an article to a *Festschrift* in his honor. I was most grateful for the opportunity that provided me the occasion for writing my first article dealing with racism and black theology that was finally published only in 2005.[11]

White Privilege

Acknowledging my failure as a Catholic theologian to recognize and deal with the problem of racism in society and the church is only the first step toward a recognition of white privilege. Shawn Copeland has rightly challenged white theologians to recognize the omnipresent reality of white privilege and how it has affected our understanding of and approach to theology. White privilege functions invisibly and systemically to confer power and privilege.[12] Only very recently have I been educated to realize the extent and power of white privilege and my participation in it.

Here too I now realize the inadequacies and errors in some of my earlier approaches. I have tried to be supportive of minority colleagues in theology. At Catholic University I purposely went out of my way to encourage African American women who were working on their doctorates. I often went to sessions of professional societies when African Americans and other minorities were presenting so that I could show my support for them.

On one occasion at a Call to Action conference I went to a session given by an African American woman theologian who was a former student. I was somewhat embarrassed because I embarrassed her. She saw me come in and sit in the last row and almost immediately told her audience that she was nervous because I had come to her session. She graciously thanked me publicly for the support I had already given her from the time that she was in graduate school.

Yes, I supported African Americans and other minority Catholic theologians, and I was quite satisfied that I was doing what I could for the cause. But only recently have I become aware of the problem with such an approach. "I" was the subject; "they" were the object. "I" was graciously doing what I could to help and support "them."

In reality, the problem was "I" and not "them." I was blithely unaware of how white privilege had shaped my understanding of what was going on. The invisible and systemic nature of white privilege came through in my absolutizing my own limited and privileged position and making all others the object of my good will. My perspective was the normative perspective from which all others were to be seen. My white theology was the theological standpoint from which all others were to be judged. I finally realized to some extent that I was the problem.

White privilege is invisible, structural, and systemic. Borrowing from Bernard Lonergan, Shawn Copeland describes white privilege as biased common sense.[13] Lonergan used the term "scotosis" to describe this reality.[14] There is a need, then, to shed light on this evil and to overcome its invisibility to the person. White privilege is a structural sin that has to be made visible and removed. Borrowing from Lonergan and Copeland, there is need for conversion and especially continuing conversion in overcoming white privilege. I have just begun to recognize white privilege as the problem, and I continually have to strive to uncover it in my own life and work. On the basis of what I have read and experienced, there are three types of conversion involved—personal, intellectual, and spiritual.

Three Conversions

With regard to the first conversion, Peggy McIntosh's seminal article is an eye-opener on the road to personal conversion.[15] I have to see myself as the oppressor and as the problem. She lists about fifty different ways in which I, as a white person, am privileged because of being white. This privilege exists in practically every aspect of my life. Making matters worse, this privilege comes at the expense of others. I have to become much more aware of the role of white privilege in my daily life brought about by the systemic injustice of racism.

I became somewhat aware of white privilege two years ago when I was teaching a course in moral theology for the Perkins School of Theology at Southern Methodist University in its Houston program. Most of the students were older and second-career folks studying for ministry. There were twenty-one students in the class, including five African Americans. In the exams and papers the African Americans received the lowest grades. But I also broke the class down into four groups to role-play different cases of quandary ethics. In this role-playing four of the African Americans truly excelled. They understood exactly what was involved, went to the heart of the case, and presented the whole issue with intelligence and humor.

The African American students in this role-playing showed themselves to be just as intelligent, and perhaps even more so, than the others in the class. But they did not have the same skills with regard to reading texts and writing papers. Obviously, they were products of a poor educational system that had never prepared them to read and write that well.

In light of that experience I reflected on my own privilege with regard to my seminary education. I was born to a family that took reading and education very seriously. My parents encouraged us to read and to get a good education. I went to good schools and had some excellent teachers. This was not all due to white privilege, but it obviously was a privilege that many others have not had.

The second conversion is intellectual. Early on I learned from Lonergan the importance of historical consciousness. The person as subject is embedded in his or her own cultural and historical environment. No one can claim to be a neutral, objective, value-free knower. Liberationist and feminist theologies made me all the more aware of social location with its limits and biases. I learned about the hermeneutic of suspicion and the need to recognize that the strong and powerful create the structures and institutions of our world. But I did not see black racism and its connection to my white privilege until I was prodded by recent writings. I was trying to help and encourage African American theologians to do their work. But I never realized how they could and should help me and my theology. My failures here indicate the need for both a stronger moral imagination and for the other conversions to affect the intellectual conversion.

The third conversion is spiritual conversion. In reading the literature I was taken by how many theologians dealing with white privilege emphasize spiritual conversion. At first I was fearful that this was an escape to reduce the invisible, structural, and systemic reality of white privilege to the realm of the spiritual. The flight to the spiritual might be a dodge for avoiding the structural and institutional realities of life.

Yes, the flight to the spiritual can be an escape, but not for one who sees the spiritual as the primary area that affects all other aspects of human existence. In moral theology I have emphasized the role of a fundamental option that gives direction to all aspects of life. But I have purposely not embraced a transcendental understanding of the fundamental option precisely because in my judgment it does not give enough importance to the historical and the concrete. The spiritual thus influences the other two conversions—the intellectual and the personal.

Here I remembered what I had forgotten for so long. In my praise of Furfey's approach, I pointed out that his Christian perspective clearly recognized the deep problems existing in American society—poverty, race, and war. The spiritual conversion of the radical Furfey made him see what others did not see.

What effect will these beginning conversions have on my doing moral theology? At this stage of my life as a "senior" theologian I am not going to become an expert on racism and white privilege. The best analogy for the future is what I have done with regard to feminist theology. I am not an expert in feminist theology, but I recognize the problem of pervasive patriarchy, I dialogue with feminism, and I have appropriated many of its insights into my own work. I hope to do the same with regard to racism and white privilege.

A spirituality that prays to a God who is black and female can and should help open my eyes to white male privilege.

Notes

[1] Charles E. Curran, *American Catholic Social Ethics: Twentieth Century Approaches* (Notre Dame, IN: University of Notre Dame Press, 1982), 149–58.

[2] Ibid., 166.

[3] Francis James Gilligan, *The Morality of the Color Line* (Washington, DC: Catholic University of America Press, 1928).

[4] Curran, *American Catholic Social Ethics*, 83.

[5] Ibid.

[6] Bryan Massingale, "The African American Experience and U.S. Roman Catholic Ethics: 'Strangers and Aliens No Longer?'" in *Black and Catholic: The Challenge and Gift of Black Folks*, ed. Jamie T. Phelps (Milwaukee: Marquette University Press, 1997), 79–101.

[7] Ibid., 94–95.

[8] Margaret Pfeil, "Option for the Poor: Dismantling White Privilege as Part of the Theological Vocation," paper presented at the

Annual Meeting of the Catholic Theological Society of America, Cincinnati, Ohio, 2003.

[9] J. Deotis Roberts, *Liberation and Reconciliation: A Black Theology* (Philadelphia: Westminster, 1971).

[10] Daniel C. Maguire, *A New American Justice: Ending the White Male Monopolies* (Garden City, NY: Doubleday, 1980).

[11] Charles E. Curran, "J. Deotis Roberts and the Roman Catholic Tradition," in *The Quest for Liberation and Reconciliation: Essays in Honor of J. Deotis Roberts*, ed. Michael Battle (Louisville, KY: Westminster/John Knox, 2005), 82–92.

[12] M. Shawn Copeland, "Racism and the Vocation of the Christian Theologian," *Spiritus* 2, no. 1 (2002), 15–29.

[13] Ibid.

[14] Bernard J. F. Lonergan, *Insight: A Study of Human Understanding* (New York: Philosophical Library, 1957), 191–203.

[15] Peggy McIntosh, "White Privilege and Male Privilege: A Personal Account of Coming to See Correspondences through Work in Women's Studies (1988)," in *Race, Class, and Gender: An Anthology*, ed. Margaret Andersen and Patricia Hill Collins, 94–105 (Albany, NY: Wadsworth Publishing, 1998).

5

• • • •

THE DYSFUNCTIONAL RHETORIC OF "WHITE PRIVILEGE" AND THE NEED FOR "RACIAL SOLIDARITY"

Roger Haight

My contribution to a discussion of white privilege in America flows directly from the fact that I am a white male. I suppose that this status accounts for the difficulty I had in formulating a statement that might be useful in this important discussion, and I still doubt whether I've succeeded. From the outset I could not clearly identify a problem I had in formulating the *status quaestionis* within the issue I sought to address. Somehow the pieces did not fit together. Only after a good deal of thought and consultation did I realize that the category of "white privilege" did not help constructively to deal with the social and cultural problems as I understood them. The burden of my input, therefore, will be to indicate why I think the phrase *dismantling white privilege* in the discussion of race relations is dysfunctional and to suggest that the phrase *racial solidarity* would be more adequate and constructive from both theological and social points of view. I am addressing a rhetorical dysfunction, a problem of communication, rather than an analysis of racism itself.

I set forth my view relatively simply in three points. In the first I describe schematically what I take Edward Schillebeeckx to mean by a negative experience of contrast. This description of the dynamics of moral experience provides the framework of my reasoning. Within that framework, then, the second point simply indicates why I think "white privilege" falls short as a rhetorical tool, and in the third, with the help of Shawn Copeland and James Cone, I suggest an alternative leading concept for the discussion.

A Negative Experience of Contrast

I suppose that most people are familiar with the idea of a "negative experience of contrast," which is so fundamental to the thinking of Edward Schillebeeckx.[1] This familiarity allows me to interpret its structure in a brief, schematic way as consisting in three elements. As I briefly list these three dimensions, imagine people all over the United States watching the evening news on their black-and-white television sets and seeing "Bull" O'Connor's police unleash dogs and fire hoses on the black men, women, and children in the streets of Birmingham as they demonstrated in the spring of 1963. With the unfolding of these events ingrained in my imagination, I describe a negative experience of contrast as consisting, first, in an experience of overt or patent negativity: something is wrong here; this should not be. Second, implicitly or explicitly, the background of the experience of negativity is positivity. Without it, the negativity would not appear as such; the negativity itself shows dialectically that there is a better way. The third dimension appears as the urge to escape, or resist, or to negate the negativity. The impulse to action is not derived by inference but lies within and is part of the experience itself. Negative experiences of contrast can be individually personal and commonplace; they can also be profound corporate experiences that change history. In fact, Birmingham was a major turning point in the civil rights movement and the history of America.

A negative experience of contrast would bear an extensive moral, epistemological analysis that I'll not engage. But I have to highlight certain qualities that will have bearing on my assessment of the concepts of white privilege and racial solidarity. The most important salient trait consists in the dialectical character of a negative experience of contrast. The positivity and negativity are not simply contrasting dimensions; they confront each other. By a dialectical quality here I mean a dynamic interaction that actually generates insight. Why is treating human beings like objects or animals wrong? Why is respect for the value of the human person right? Further, the interaction of the negative and the positive actively generates the impulse to action, which in turn takes its energy from the need for good to triumph over evil. A negative experience of contrast is moving.

It is also deep. One can follow a significant negative experience of contrast down through its roots by transcendental analysis to the need of some guarantor of human values or some deeper ground of moral coherence. When the assessment of human life itself is at stake, the moral shades into the theological, and one finds oneself asking questions of ultimacy. Beneath all the strategies of prophecy and utopia that one finds in liberation theologies, and all the tactics of denouncing and announcing, lies a negative experience of contrast and of its dialectics. Its theological depth is revealed in all discussions of the prophetic and the mystical and how they relate to each other ultimately, that is, theologically.

To conclude this first point, the moral-theological structure of a negative experience of contrast provides the horizon within which I want to make some suggestions about the language of white privilege.

The Rhetorical Dysfunctionality of the Category White Privilege

The concept of white privilege, as realistic as it may be in describing a force that inhibits justice in the ongoing social relationships between races, does not function well in a language that might be used to ameliorate those relationships. To show why I think that to be the case, I will use the concept of white privilege as it is developed by Peggy McIntosh and criticize it against the background of Schillebeeckx's contrast experience.[2]

The first general defining description is that white privilege is "an invisible package of unearned assets that I can count on cashing in each day, but about which I was 'meant' to remain oblivious. White privilege is like an invisible weightless knapsack of special provisions" (94–95). A number of characteristics tighten the focus: white privilege is unearned since one is born into it; it is shallow and only skin deep. White privilege is systemic, institutionalized, embedded in social cultural patterns (95). Those who possess the privilege are unconscious of its oppressiveness relative to those who do not and thus frequently fail to acknowledge it. They take it as the normal pattern and think that others should share it too, without cost to their own position (95–96).

The phenomenology of white privilege reveals some distinctions between kinds of conditioning that are more or less oppressive. I note three of these. First, some forms of privilege are in fact "what one would want for everyone in a just society" (100) and thus one should wish that all shared the privilege so that it were not a privilege. In that case the sentiment of wishing that others would be "more like 'us'" (96) in sharing the privilege would be a condescending but not unreasonable response and presumably without cost. A second group of privileges is those held over against other groups: they provide advantages or "over-empower" in what otherwise would be a more level playing field. In a competitive world of limited resources this privilege may disadvantage others, and surrendering it may involve cost. Still a third form of systemic white privileges is aggressively hostile to others; this pattern of valuing and acting "*confers dominance*, gives permission to control, because of one's race" (101). Here white privilege "gives license to some people to be, at best, thoughtless and, at worst, murderous" toward other groups (101).[3]

The case I want to make against the category of white privilege concerns its functionality in the public rhetoric of social reconstruction. I thus support the descriptive and analytical accuracy of the phrase, but I question its usefulness in public language that urges reform.

To begin, the analysis of white privilege succeeds in raising to a conscious level mechanisms that might otherwise be invisible. It helps to lay bare and explain certain objective situations in which the rights and persons of blacks are suppressed by various practices that in fact entail the myth of white supremacy and domination. It describes the conflict between races as socially and culturally systemic. The category of white privilege does not add anything to an objective analysis of racism, which intrinsically is "systematized oppression of one race by another."[4] But it contains a certain power and sharpness by highlighting and dwelling on the role of whites in the racist situation. Moreover, its analysis does not place emphasis on the historical origins of the problem but concentrates attention on the deep social-psychological roots that obtain in the present. The category of white privilege shifts the focus of a more objective analysis of racism and a description of its negative effects to white subjects and thereby underlines white ideology, responsibility, and inactivity.

If all this sounds right, why is the category of white privilege dysfunctional? Several reasons contribute to this judgment. Generally the category is intended as negative; white privilege is not a good thing. But in fact the majority of instances that McIntosh lists are not materially negative or evil, for they are, as she notes, sometimes normal human expectations or legal rights in a just society. Their negative side lies in the privilege, the formality that other groups are deprived of them. This leads to the conclusion that the negativity of what are called white privileges is at least ambiguous until the category is more carefully differentiated.

Second, the relationship between what may be called a white privilege and its absence in other groups is uneven. Sometimes there is a causal relationship between what are internalized as white privileges and the oppression of blacks; this is especially clear when privileges include dominative values or vices, or when they bestow unfair advantage in a competitive situation. But in many of the examples there is no such direct relationship, and this is indicated by the fact that the desire that others participate in these privileges requires absolutely no self-transcendence. In short, an undifferentiated category of white privilege unevenly assigns responsibility or blame to whites for the deprivations of blacks. This unevenness acquires some importance because it partially explains the source of the rhetorical dysfunction.

Third, the language of white privilege has failed on a rhetorical level to be generative in white segments of society. Its dysfunctionality lies in the ambiguity of the non-differentiated term *white privilege*. It occurs especially in an appeal to action that at best lacks nuance, to "dismantling white privilege," which often seems to attack the material content of the rights that blacks themselves aspire to. The problem relative to whites consists in the perception that this is non-dialectical language; it does not appeal to a higher goal for action that arises out of the tension between negativity and positivity. "Dismantling white privilege" is denunciation without annunciation, prophecy without utopia. It focuses the problem on whites in a negative, accusatory way without a positive, constructive, or visionary horizon.

Let me sum up the argument thus far. The dysfunction that I am addressing is rhetorical; the phrase *dismantling structures of white privilege* does not communicate what one would wish the social analysis would lead to, namely, a movement toward social amelioration. On the one hand, I readily agree with the description of white privilege; the descriptive phenomenology is accurate. But, on the other hand, it is an objectively ambiguous category and conceptually adds nothing to what is described and characterized as racism. Analysis of racism and analysis of white privilege are the same thing; an understanding of racism is an understanding of white privilege; white privilege is racism. These points help explain why, subjectively, the category will fail to move people toward a resolution of the problem. This is the burden of the next part of this essay.

Racial Solidarity

I move to a more constructive phase of this discussion with the suggestion that a positive concept of racial solidarity would be more fruitful in the discussion of racism than the negative category of white privilege. In making this case I draw into the conversation the voices of Schillebeeckx, Shawn Copeland, and James Cone. I make the case in three stages. First, the logic of a negative experience of contrast transcends racial differentiation. Second, the way to build on that foundational experience must be a positive and inclusive language of shared goals. Third, this logic is illustrated by Cone's analysis of the structure of the civil rights movement.

To begin, the epistemological dynamics of a negative experience of contrast are such that it rests on no premises; it is not a conclusion but a direct, intuitive perception and judgment. Obviously, blacks experience the negativity more directly and intensely than whites. But a realistic descriptive account of racism and its effects can and does elicit a negative experience of contrast that is universally available because what is being attacked is a common humanity. A description of racism and a recognition of various degrees of systemic dehumanization of blacks can be a shared human experience, that is, one that transcends blacks and is able to be appreciated by whites and by all. It is an autonomous, noncompetitive experience. The analysis of the situation and especially the conception of how one is to react to, resist, or aggressively fight the negativity easily gives way to a variety of different analyses based on perspective and self-interest. But this intensifies the need to stress and build upon the commonality of the basic negative experience of contrast; cooperative resistance requires a constructive concept that is both positive and shared by all. The problem requires categories that draw people together so that a common desire for resistance may develop and with it an ability to discuss a variety of ways to attach the objective situation.

Second, the utopian dimension of a concept of human solidarity implied in a negative experience of racism corresponds with common values in American society and culture, with common human ideals in an increasingly globalized world culture, and with basic Christian premises and ideals, without being overtly denominational. Implied in a concept of human solidarity is racial solidarity. I will develop this idea in terms suggested by Shawn Copeland.[5]

Copeland develops the idea of solidarity in an essay on a feminist theology of solidarity that tries to overcome any competition between white, Latina, and black or womanist theologies. Strategically one can only arrive at such a notion by mutual listening to the story of the other and by social analysis. Such a notion of solidarity will be built on several elements. It requires acknowledgment of the interconnection of oppressions and forms of dehumanization; "they impinge on each other and mutually condition each other. These oppressions cannot be reduced or collapsed into one another."[6] Further, solidarity is built upon a common anthropology. It requires an appeal to the *humanum*, a common human good; it cannot allow race, or gender, or class interests to supersede what we share in common.[7] Moreover, solidarity is an achievement of community; it is not individualist or the achievement of a single group over against others. Community is precisely a group of mutually affirming autonomous selves, individuals committed to mutuality. Insofar as one is thinking in terms of Christian theology, "solidarity is grounded in the confession of Jesus as Lord."[8]

The idea of "striving for racial solidarity" does not function in the same manner as "dismantling white privilege," which simply compounds the negativity of racism itself. Rather it rises out of the dialectic between racial injustice and its negation as something out in front of us. It represents what could and should be as a utopian goal for which all can strive. It does not isolate whites and render them defensive of their interests over against blacks but rather appeals to a common humanitarian interest and to Christian self-transcendence in the interest of the common good and community. It also appeals to American civil religious values and legal ideals enshrined in the Constitution. It provides a concrete positive goal for human striving for something that easily correlates with the religious motivation symbolized by the Christian metaphor of the kingdom of God.

To recapitulate my thesis, the first section of the discussion, setting up the structure of a negative experience of contrast, establishes the need for mediating a dialectical perception of social evil in order to gain the motivation to resist. If language is only denunciatory, it will not provide the very perception that is needed to foster the motivation to resist. For example, the phrase *racism and white privilege* contains no dialectical tension but only pleonasm or redundancy. Sometimes that is good, and it serves rhetorically to emphasize something. But it lacks the dialectical binary of negative-positive that will move people to action; it is rather a binary of negative and more negativity. Therefore, I propose that the analysis of racism be accompanied by a language of racial solidarity as the positivity of what should be and can be if human beings strive for it. As long as social rhetoric uses only prophetic language of denunciation without a dialectically related language of what should and can be, it will not communicate or connect but probably engender a reaction opposite to what is intended. What is intended is resistance to the evil situation and mobilization of human energies; an analysis of racism that is accusation will more likely engender a hardening of spirit.

Finally, I want to bring James Cone's analysis of the logic of the civil rights movement during the 1950s and 1960s to bear on this discussion.[9] Once again I place his thesis over against the background of the scene in Birmingham in the spring of 1963. Cone presents his case with an analysis of the thought and practice of Martin Luther King Jr. and Malcolm X. These figures stand symbolically for two rhetorics and strategies relative to race relations that are intimately united in their common cause of racial justice for African Americans; at certain points, however, they diverge and are diametrically opposed. On the one hand, King espoused the "American dream" of an integrated society; on the other hand, Malcolm, speaking of the "nightmare" of black Americans, wanted to burn white America as inherently hostile to black people. Cone shows how both of these languages bear truth and how toward the end each began to move closer to the other, but that, finally, these are two distinct dimensions of a strategy that must include both in a complementing and mutually correcting tension. I associate the "white privilege" language with prophetic language relative to whites in the line of Malcolm X, and I associate "racial solidarity" language with Martin Luther King's dream. In Cone's synthesis these two dimensions must subsist together and in tension. But the overarching, synthetic framework lies with King, for the practical reason that blacks and whites have to live together, and for the theoretical reason that this represents the higher good in terms that are humanitarian, American, and Christian. In sum, the concept of racial solidarity suggests a rhetoric of common participatory action for a shared utopian dream in the pattern of Martin Luther King Jr.

Notes

¹ The following sources are helpful for reconstructing Schillebeeckx's negative experience of contrast: Edward Schillebeeckx, *God the Future of Man* (New York: Sheed and Ward, 1968), 153–54; *Jesus: An Experiment in Christology* (New York: Seabury, 1979), 621–22; *The Understanding of Faith: Interpretation and Criticism* (New York: Seabury, 1974), 91–101; *Church: The Human Story of God* (New York: Crossroad, 1990), 5–6; Patricia McAuliffe, *Fundamental Ethics: A Liberationist Approach* (Washington, DC: Georgetown University Press, 1993), 1–38; Kathleen Anne McManus, *Unbroken Communion: The Place and Meaning of Suffering in the Theology of Edward Schillebeeckx* (Lanham, MD: Rowman and Littlefield, 2003).

² Peggy McIntosh, "White Privilege and Male Privilege: A Personal Account of Coming to See Correspondences through Work in Women's Studies (1988)," in *Race, Class, and Gender: An Anthology*, ed. Margaret Andersen and Patricia Hill Collins (Albany, NY: Wadsworth Publishing, 1998), 94–105. References in the text are to pages of this essay.

³ McIntosh makes or implicitly raises up other distinctions along the way. Active forms of white privilege overtly discriminate as they

are acted out while other more passive-aggressive forms lie hidden. Some patterned privileges may be so embedded in a society or culture and internalized by all that they are taken for granted (104).

⁴ M. Shawn Copeland, "Racism and the Vocation of the Christian Theologian," *Spiritus* 2 (2002): 16, citing James Boggs. Racism is so embedded in social relationships that it becomes part of them and individuals are scarcely aware of the way they function. It is a structured or institutionalized pattern of behavior "carried forward through unquestioned acceptance and affirmation of standards, symbols, habits, reactions, and practices rooted in racial differentiation and racist privilege implicit in the creation and transmission of culture."

⁵ I draw Copeland's characterization of racial solidarity from M. Shawn Copeland, "Toward a Critical Christian Feminist Theology of Solidarity," in *Women and Theology*, ed. Mary Ann Hinsdale and Phyllis H. Kaminski (Maryknoll, NY: Orbis Books, 1995), 3–38.

⁶ Ibid., 28.

⁷ Ibid., 29.

⁸ Copeland appeals to the concept of the body of Christ as the doctrinal grounds of solidarity and feminist theology: "Thus, we are called to be active members of the Body of Christ, living as Jesus lived, subordinating our personal and collective, social and cultural decisions to the coming Reign of God" (31). Solidarity demands or entails self-transcendence, and thus it requires transcendent empowerment. Copeland retrieves the theology of the mystical body of Christ to reinforce the conception of union in love within the church against what diminishes and dehumanizes. This doctrine stands for the currents of love that undergird the Christian vision of reality, beginning with the Trinity and descending through Christ and the Spirit to constitute a community of self-transcending love in action. "The Mystical Body of Christ is an eschatological reality; it is anticipated in the here-and-now through the gift of grace. To grasp our being in the world as the Mystical Body is to enact a praxis of solidarity that both forwards the *humanum* in poor women of color and enfolds the repentance of white male bourgeois Europeans" (M. Shawn Copeland, "The New Anthropological Subject at the Heart of the Mystical Body of Christ," *Proceedings of the Catholic Theological Society of America* 53 [1998]: 46).

⁹ James H. Cone, *Martin and Malcolm: A Dream or a Nightmare?* (Maryknoll, NY: Orbis Books, 1991).

6

• • • •

MORAL IMAGINATION
AND THE *MISSIO AD GENTES*

Redressing the Counter-Witness of Racism

Margaret E. Guider

Granting the centrality of the missionary mandate in the life of the church[1] and acknowledging the permanent validity of the missionary vocation,[2] this chapter examines one of the major obstacles impeding the *missio ad gentes,* namely the counter-witness of Christians.[3] In this chapter I identify the multifaceted phenomenon of racism as an insidious problem throughout the world and posit the continued complicity of Christians in the perpetuation of racist attitudes, behaviors, social structures, and ideologies as a primary impediment to evangelization. In short, I argue that racism is one of the most serious forms of counter-witness to the gospel.

Considering the church's expressed commitment to "form consciences by revealing to people the . . . equality of all men and women as God's sons and daughters,"[4] I observe that in advancing the *missio ad gentes* the church acts in ways that reveal the embeddedness of some of its leaders and members in the sinful

This is a revision of an article titled "White Privilege and Racism" published in the *Proceedings of the Catholic Theological Society of America* 57 (2002): 132.

structures of racism. Whenever the church fails, refuses, or is unable or afraid to allow its own moral imagination to be engaged and transformed by the efforts of those who dare to confront racist forms of counter-witness, the very credibility of the gospel message it seeks to proclaim is undermined.

In an effort to demonstrate the moral urgency of confronting this counter-witness, I propose a thought experiment in moral imagination and the *missio ad gentes* as a point of reference for theological reflection on racism and white superiority. This thought experiment takes seriously the scandal of the racist counter-witness of many adult followers of Jesus and its effects on yet another generation of children. In doing so, this theological exercise in moral imagination looks to children as both supporters and subjects of Christian mission as well as the most vulnerable victims of racism and the most compelling protagonists for racial justice.

Focusing on the exigencies of the reign of God as articulated and embodied by Jesus in his own turn to the child, I draw attention to this often overlooked vision and criterion for understanding proclamation and reception. In the light of this vision and criterion, I conclude by raising a question about the measure of our own courage and insight as theologians and interpreters of the *missio Dei*.

Christian Mission:
Coming to Terms with the
Multifaceted Phenomenon of Racism

On the post-modern horizon of paradox and ambiguity, the missionary moratorium debates[5] rage on, the *pax et iustitia* vs. *missio ad gentes* controversies continue, and the dangerous memories of the consequences of muscular Christianity encounter the bold and humble visions of the often vulnerable yet courageous followers of Jesus. In this crucible of religious, social, cultural, political, and economic consciousness, missionaries are often catalysts for ecclesial transformation inasmuch as theological reflection on their experiences and insights serve to form and inform the moral imagination of the church and, oftentimes, the world.

From the early beginnings of the church until today, the example, testimony, and influence of Christian missionaries has been characterized on the one hand as edifying and on the other hand as scandalous. Some are remembered for their compassion, insight, and commitment. Others are remembered for their contentious behavior, competing claims, and devastating tactics. For centuries, ethical reflection on the witness and counter-witness of missionaries has compelled the community of believers to come to terms with the interactive dynamics of faith and history, of gospel and culture, and of religion and race.[6] Such reflection, however, has been, is, and will continue to be both demanding and dangerous. It is demanding inasmuch as it requires Christians to constantly reexamine who we understand ourselves to be in relationship to God, the world, others, and ourselves. It is dangerous because it requires all of us who count ourselves among the followers of Jesus to live with dangerous and demanding questions, particularly those unsettling and soul-searching questions that make it difficult for us to be at ease in our old dispensations.

Admittedly, when it comes to responding to the call to live with the questions raised by ethical reflection on missionary activity in faith, hope, love, and truth, the temptation to deny, suppress, or censor the questions that trouble our still waters is a powerful one. Unwilling or unable to go where these questions might lead, some of us are drawn by the seductive appeal of absolutism, presumption, indifference, and false consciousness. Unwilling or unable to bear the burden of these questions any longer, some of us yield to the fatal attraction of doubt, despair, contempt, and amnesia. The vices of the idols of death rival the virtues bestowed by the God of Life (see Table 6–1). Nowhere is succumbing to temptation more evident than in our failure, refusal, inability, or fear to live with the troubling questions concerning the role of Christians in general and missionaries in

Table 6-1

Absolutism	FAITH	Doubt
Presumption	HOPE	Despair
Indifference	LOVE	Contempt
False consciousness	TRUTH	Amnesia

particular in causing, contributing to, and exacerbating human suffering and oppression.

To the extent that racist attitudes, behaviors, and habits of the heart may be ranked among the most serious forms of counter-witness to the message of Jesus, I contend that the multifaceted reality of racism remains a major obstacle to the proclamation and reception of the gospel.[7] Furthermore, it is an obstacle that is both veiled and visible. I would argue further that, in terms of the human suffering it has caused and continues to cause, it is of far greater moral consequence than other obstacles that often command far more attention from church leaders and theologians, such as missionary malaise and theological relativism.

Inasmuch as proclamation and all that it entails continue to be understood by the church as the permanent priority of the *missio ad gentes*,[8] moral responsibility for promoting racial justice by redressing and eradicating racism is undeniably one of the primary ethical imperatives of mission. Practically speaking, this means that the church, in the process of proclaiming the good news to people of every land and nation, needs to continually remind itself of one important fact. Efforts at inculturation, on the part of missionaries and, by extension, all those who participate in Christ's mission to communicate the gospel message effectively, are exceedingly important, but they are not sufficient. Though truth and goodness may be found and abound through inculturation, racism and white superiority will not be exorcised unless they are called by name.

Given the realities of our world, something more is required of all Christians and, in particular, of all missionaries. This something more involves going beyond the offering of warrants for and affirmations of the value and integrity of every human person. It goes beyond the valorization of cultures and histories. This something more requires us to render a constant and consistent evangelical witness that acknowledges, identifies, confesses, redresses, and prevents racism, along with its multiple causes, consequences, and manifestations in the world and within the church.[9] When and if the church does not do this of its own volition, the moral forces at work within the world have and will compel it to do so.

Redressing and Eradicating White Superiority and All Forms of Racism in the New Millennium: The Problem, the Sin, and the Obstacle to the *Missio ad Gentes*

On August 31, 2001, during the year declared by the United Nations as the International Year of Dialogue among Civilizations, the World Conference on Racism, Racial Discrimination, Xenophobia, and Related Intolerance convened in Durban, South Africa.[10] Drawing the attention of the world, the conference created an arena of discourse and dialogue about racism and racial justice in a global context. Proceedings from preparatory regional gatherings as well as pre-conference statements issued by a number of countries and nongovernmental organizations presented both negative and positive observations about missionaries in particular and Christians in general.[11]

On the one hand, these findings attest to the fact that the legacy of Western Christian missionary activity continues to be identified as a historical and contemporary factor in the exacerbation of racism, xenophobia, and other forms of discrimination based on race and ethnicity. Among the most unsettling criticisms are those raised by cultural survival groups that call into question the sincerity of apologies offered in recent years by church leaders for atrocities committed in the past against indigenous peoples. They cite examples of Christian missionaries who are currently taking part in similar atrocities against indigenous peoples in the north of Thailand and in Amazonia.[12] Their conclusions are condemnatory of church leaders who have made apologies and offered token reparations for misguided zeal, ignorance, abuse, and exaggerations on the part of missionaries. They question why individuals and groups of missionaries who engage in the same reprehensible forms of proselytism that gave rise to the need for apologies and reparations in the first place continue to be commissioned. The conclusion drawn by these international observers is that some Christian churches do not seem to learn from their acknowledged mistakes and must be held accountable for the violations of human rights associated with the activities of missionaries.

On the other hand, observers also take note of the positive contributions made by Christian leaders, some of whom are expatriate missionaries, who have offered substantial support and ongoing guidance in national, regional, and international efforts to bring about racial justice, reparations, and reconciliation in places such as South Africa, Guatemala, and East Timor. In a similar fashion, international recognition of the efforts made by Christian leaders to address racism and other forms of discrimination have been viewed as a source of hope and encouragement to many national, regional, and global agencies, particularly those that endeavor to emphasize the positive resources that the religions of the world bring to the promotion of human rights and the defense of human dignity.[13]

Whether intended or unintended, the World Conference on Racism created the necessary conditions for raising consciousness and eliciting accountability from Christian leaders at the beginning of the twenty-first century. It set in motion a revisiting of the questions that have troubled many Christian missionaries and missionary-sending societies for over four decades and longer. The World Conference on Racism also posed new questions to Christian leaders and missionaries. In the process, the conference evoked from Roman Catholic leaders, among others, a renewed commitment to articulate pastoral statements about racism and plans of action for placing and keeping racial justice at the center of mission and ministry in the post-modern context.

Racism as a Problem in the World

In 1978, UNESCO declared:

> Any theory which involves the claim that racial or ethnic groups are inherently superior or inferior, thus implying that some would be entitled to dominate or eliminate others, presumed to be inferior, or which bases value judgments on racial differentiation, has no scientific foundation and is contrary to the moral and ethical principles of humanity.

Nearly three decades later, despite the best efforts of UNESCO and other worldwide agencies, impressionistic evidence from around the globe suggests that racism, like other forms of structural oppression, is alive and well and rampant just about everywhere, having evolved into an ever more violent, dehumanizing, and demonizing phenomenon.

Racism, understood as a system by which one race maintains supremacy over another race through a set of attitudes, behaviors, social structures, ideologies, and the requisite power needed to impose them, is far from being eliminated or eradicated. Defined as a social problem by governmental and nongovernmental entities alike, it may rise and fall in arenas of social and political consciousness, but it does not go away. Though the contexts where racism manifests itself may differ, the dynamics of racism are all too similar. Racist practices of oppression, marginalization, and exclusion, whether based on skin color or cultural, ethnic, and physical differences, continue to legitimate many forms of bigotry, discrimination, abuse, and violence.

Speaking from within the contexts of North America and Europe, racism has been largely understood as a system of white supremacy and white superiority. These words fall heavy on the ears of white Christians as we scramble to distinguish ourselves from men in white hoods or brown shirts or youths with Confederate flags, shaved heads, and swastika tattoos. As the grandchildren and great-grandchildren of immigrants, refugees, and exiles, our appeals to our poor and peasant European roots do not alter the fact that we are the white-skinned beneficiaries of the very system we repudiate. To the extent that ecclesiastical power structures continue to be largely under the direction of the descendants of Europeans, the power to make and enforce decisions continues to be in their hands. They set the standards of behavior considered to be normative, if not superior, and these standards continue to be those by which the behaviors of other groups are judged. When talking about racism, the descendants of European immigrants often define reality incorrectly. As the beneficiaries of racism, they fail to understand that the "problem" tends to be constructed in ways that repeatedly overlook the dynamics of racial privilege.[14]

These observations are not new. They have been around for quite some time. Nevertheless, it is important to remember that history and culture—global and ecclesiastical—have not remained static since 1968. In fact, it can be argued that globalization has effectively intensified the Euro-Americanization of world culture, which subsequently has led to permutations of racism as seen, for example, in internalized racism and cross-racial hostilities. The former "occurs in a racist system when an oppressed race supports the supremacy of the dominating race through maintaining or participating in the set of attitudes, behaviors, social structures and ideologies that undergird that supremacy."[15] The latter "occurs in a racist system when one oppressed race supports the oppression of another oppressed race by maintaining or participating in the set of attitudes, behaviors, social structures, and ideologies that underlie the dominating race's supremacy."[16]

And so, the multifaceted and insidious problem of racism continues to take a toll on human life and human relationships throughout the world. Often justified by the manipulation of religious beliefs and the tacit approval of religious leaders, the phenomenon of racism all too often remains impervious to ethical scrutinies and investigations of human-rights violations. This situation has made it difficult for all religions, and Christianity in particular, to take full account of their complicity of silence, fear, and indifference when confronted with the modern and postmodern manifestations of a social evil of such magnitude.

Racism as a Sin in the Church

The twentieth-century record of Roman Catholic statements dealing with the realities of racism, discrimination, and prejudice is worthy of separate analysis as a case study in promulgation and reception.[17] Papal statements[18] and statements by Vatican commissions,[19] along with pastoral letters of national and regional episcopal conferences,[20] local bishops and diocesan commissions,[21] and documents of religious institutes and Catholic lay organizations provide more than sufficient evidence of clearly articulated theological and moral positions on racism as a sin. Statements and formal declarations are made with regularity and intentionality.[22]

If, however, the measure of the church's success in effectively communicating its ideals is to be measured in terms of social transformation, rather than numbers of carefully drafted documents, the overwhelming evidence suggests a lack of adequate promulgation. The evidence also suggests a limited broad-based reception of church teaching and a lack of persuasive, convincing, consistent, and coherent pastoral practices. Outward visible signs of living in the truth upon which reparations, reconciliation, and the prevention of racism are predicated, while observable, are unfortunately few and far between.

Recognizing and acknowledging racism as a sin is a confession that has not come easily to many sectors of the Christian community. In this regard, resistance from perpetrators, beneficiaries, and bystanders has curtailed action on behalf of justice. Admitting that racism is both a personal and a social sin that individual Christians have committed and in which Christians have been complicit has been a long time in coming. Nonetheless, it has occurred. Confessing racism as a sin for which the Roman Catholic Church—as church—is guilty, however, has not occurred. As the bride of Christ, the admission of such guilt is not possible for the church theologically and symbolically. This is, in part, because Jesus Christ as head of the church is not guilty and in part because the church is also made up of members who have experienced the consequences of racism as the victims, survivors, and protagonists of racial justice. As for the guilt of those who have been the perpetrators and beneficiaries of racism, there is a collective dimension to our sin that cannot be mitigated by simply ascribing culpability to individuals.

Inasmuch as the church is made up of perpetrators, victims, beneficiaries, bystanders, protagonists, offenders, and offended, what does the authentic voice of the church sound like when it speaks out against racism? I would venture to say that much of the world has yet to hear that voice. With some exceptions ecclesial statements on racism tend to reveal a church that is self-referentially white and speaks in a white voice.[23] So it would seem that if it may be possible to hear the voice of the white church speaking and visualize the white church acting in and through these documents on racism, the holy yet sinful white church of history must be more than a figment of the imagination. To be more precise, there must be some way for this white church of history collectively to acknowledge its counter-witness to the gospel before the world, confess its sin to the church of faith, ask for forgiveness, and do penance.

Racism as an Obstacle to the *Missio ad Gentes*

Given the ethical imperatives that the Roman Catholic Church faces in the new millennium, our moral imagination must help us to create a space within the Roman Catholic Church of faith for the white church of history to become a confessing church.[24] I readily acknowledge the problematic aspects of this notion for Roman Catholic ecclesiology inasmuch as the invisible church is distinguished from the visible. The seeming impossibility of addressing collective guilt on the part of white Roman Catholics, however, is also problematic. There is nothing, however, except an act of will, preventing those of us who are white Catholic theologians from making such a confession, not only out of obligation, but as a authentic sign that we are, it is to be hoped, growing in virtue—in response to the signs of times and God's grace. In advancing the position that racism is a primary obstacle to the *missio ad gentes*, I want to emphasize that envisioning such an action on our part would be only an initial step, albeit a potentially significant one. I use the qualifier "potentially significant" advisedly because the degree to which such an action will actually bring about the social transformation this proposal envisions is tenuous and uncertain at best. Indeed, it could be an important step in a much larger ecclesial process of revealing and redressing racism and white superiority as major obstacles to the *missio ad gentes* and to doing the kind of theology that our church and the world both need and seek.

Beyond collectively confessing our participation in the sin of racism, such an action could take us from the realm of moral discourse to that of moral agency, if in fact we would give ourselves over to the undertaking of genuine acts of repentance. Though such actions could cost us nothing less than everything, I dare say that they could offer us an unprecedented opportunity as well. Such an opportunity, more commonly known as an occasion of grace, might enable us to discover or recover the core of our vocation as theologians, a vocation that among other responsibilities involves not only talking about but actually removing the obstacles that impede people's access to the truth revealed in the gospel message of Jesus Christ.

What I am proposing here is not a new idea. Rather, it represents an effort to review a chapter in the personal histories of Roman Catholic theologians that is often lost or forgotten and which, given the exigencies of our time, merits recovery. Indeed, there are individuals who centuries or decades ago anticipated the need for taking action against racism, while recognizing and admitting their own complicity in a sinful structure.

Among the white Roman Catholic theological voices of the latter part of the twentieth century that perceived racism to be an obstacle to the church's efforts to fulfill the mission entrusted to it, we find several names.[25] The example of each theologian's life reveals that taking up topics such as racism and anti-Semitism involves many challenges, not the least of which is the fact that attending to one form of structural oppression inevitably leads to the recognition of its interconnectedness with other forms. They remind us that whenever theologians upset the equilibrium of the status quo by seeking accountability from civil and ecclesiastical authorities, urging their theological colleagues to recognize the ways in which the Bible and tradition have been manipulated in order to justify sinful structures, or challenging Christians to acknowledge their individual and collective participation in sinful structures and habits of the heart, we do so knowing the possible consequences.

Tracing the life trajectories of white Roman Catholic theologians who responded to the call to reflect theologically, ecclesiologically, and morally on racism and white superiority over the course of the past fifty years leads to some important observations and relevant insights in terms of what they actually did and what we, too, are called to do.

Committing themselves to the task of examining the biblical and theological underpinnings of counter-witness and its implications for mission and ministry, locally and globally, these theologians offered an example to their colleagues, their students, and church leaders:

- They took account of the broader implications of racism for evangelization and the *missio ad gentes*.
- They contributed to creating the conditions for sharing space with theologians of many races and cultures, perhaps

imperfectly and not without creating other problems and tensions in the process. Nonetheless, they participated in the process, knowing that one of its consequences would be the requisite "de-centering" of their own voices, visions, and insights in the theological arena of discourse for the sake of the gospel and the future of the church.

• They placed a priority on naming and confronting the reality of white supremacy, white superiority, and white privilege and infused this consciousness into their subsequent works.

• They engaged in theological investigation and reflection on other forms of structural oppression including neocolonial imperialism, capitalism, sexism, militarism, religious absolutism, destruction of the environment, and the historical abuse of power in the church.

• They contributed to a renewed understanding of the fact that theology could not be done in isolation or as a series of monologues. Rather, theology had to be predicated on dialogue, on engagement with the world, on fidelity, conscience, integrity, creativity, and historical consciousness.

In recognizing racism as a root evil, a sin of incredible proportions, they joined their voices with those oppressed by racism. Endeavoring, though not always succeeding, to address the racism that filtered into their own ways of thinking and acting, they touched the conscience of the church, the academy, and society as they called for a deeper integration of theological imagination and moral imagination in the service of racial justice. The irony in all of this is that the theological reflection for which they may most be remembered is usually not the work they did on racism. Accounting for this fact is certainly a point that merits more detailed investigation and analysis. For the purposes of this essay, however, suffice it to say that recalling their example serves as a means for understanding the relevance of moral imagination for the ongoing reflection on the *missio ad gentes* and the reality of racism. It also alerts us to the forces that prevail in the church, in the academy, and in society with regard to the selection process that determines the contents of theological legacies.

Moral Imagination and the *Missio ad Gentes*: A Thought Experiment

In describing the dynamics of moral imagination, Sharon Parks observes that "people imagine their world into being. We compose what we find. The imagination orients one to choose and notice certain details over countless others. The imagination then informs the way in which one makes sense of the details, forming patterns out of disparate elements. In other words, it acts first as a kind of filter and then as a kind of lens."[26] In accord with this description, I suggest that as theologians, we, too, imagine our world into being and compose what we find. We choose and notice details, we make sense of them, and we form patterns. What begins as a filter turns into a lens. And so it is with this reflection.

Early on, I made the claim that racist behaviors, attitudes, and habits of the heart are a counter-witness to the gospel of Jesus Christ and, as such, obstacles to both proclamation and reception. I also noted that missionary malaise and religious relativism tend to preoccupy some church leaders concerned with the *missio ad gentes* far more than the problem of racism. Perhaps this is because missionary malaise and religious relativism are more of a preoccupation for the white church of history as it ponders what its place and legacy will be in the already emerged world church of faith and history.

Or, could it be that much of the contentiousness in Roman Catholic theological discourse today is in fact a manifestation of veiled yet pervasive forms of white superiority and other forms of racism, including internalized racism and cross-racial hostility, that continue to obstruct and impede the *missio ad gentes* in ways that none of us fully comprehend? Does the conscious conflict that we experience in discussions of the *missio ad gentes* disclose some of our own uneasiness with regard to our actual participation in the *missio Dei*?[27] Is this uneasiness elicited from a sense that something is not fitting as we take into account what the church claims and what the historical record shows? As we ask these questions, it is important to remember that at the outset of the twenty-first century, missionary activity is not only in the hands of missionaries from Western Europe and North

America, but also in the hands of increasing numbers of missionaries from other regions of the world.

Mindful of this fact, it is important to underscore that four decades of theological reflection on various aspects of the *missio ad gentes* have been shaped by the interactive dynamics of theological curiosity, the devastating shattering of theological assumptions, a vague theological restlessness, an intense weariness of things as they are in the world and in the church, a body of broken theological and ecclesiological expectations, a coming to terms with intra-ecclesial, inter-ecclesial, and interreligious conflict, and the discovery of theological dissonance.[28] At the same time theological reflection on mission has been shaped by the spiritual resiliency of unrelenting reconcilers; the courageous testimony of witnesses of faith and hope; and the creative, constructive, and compassionate visions of unwavering protagonists for peace, justice, dialogue, and solidarity.[29] Indeed, theological reflection on the *missio ad gentes* has brought to the attention of the church and its leaders the moral significance of this unprecedented *kairos* moment.

If my analysis of the role that racism plays in obstructing and impeding the *missio ad gentes* is correct, there is a way in which the landscape of what has been characterized as the "new springtime" for mission[30] must also be understood as a metaphorical minefield. Perhaps many of us would prefer to avoid this landscape/minefield altogether, rather than risk our lives and limbs embarking on a task of finding and defusing the landmines of racism before they maim and kill the souls of another generation of unsuspecting children of every race and culture. To the extent that those who placed the landmines, whether long ago or recently, have no recollection of when they were buried, where they were buried, or how many there really are, the task is all the more difficult and dangerous. Covered over by new vegetation, lush, green, and beautiful, the difficulties and dangers are compounded.

But this is no time for theologians to lack courage or creativity. Rather, it is time for us to place our theological, moral, and missiological imaginations at the service of proclamation in unanticipated and as yet unimagined ways. In an effort to consider the moral imperative that is at the heart of this chapter—namely, the moral urgency of acting for the sake of the child and with children—I would like to propose a thought experiment that involves taking a turn to the child, a turn that requires us to consider the child as a benefactor of the *missio ad gentes* as well as its subject, not as an object, and, ultimately, as one of the world's most vulnerable victims of racist ideology and one of the gospel's most persuasive protagonists for racial justice.

Turning to the Child:
A Case Study in Children's Participation
in the *Missio ad Gentes*

I begin by proposing that the formation of the moral imagination of cradle Roman Catholics begins in childhood and that part of that formation involves identity formation, consciousness raising, and the inculcation of responsibility for a larger world and a world church. Key to this process has been what, for lack of a more precise term, is called mission education. Elements of this phenomenon can be traced to the dawning of the missionary era in the sixteenth century. However, it was the European missionary movements of the mid-nineteenth century and the North American missionary endeavors of the early twentieth century that contributed to the development and intensification of children as sponsors of the *missio ad gentes and* children as the subjects of the *missio ad gentes*.

Many missionary-sending societies organized children's campaigns in Europe and North America, ostensibly to support the evangelization and humanitarian care of children in regions of the world designated by the Vatican as mission territories. The establishment of the Holy Childhood Association in 1843 by Bishop Charles de Forbin-Janson in Nancy, France, marked the beginning of this children's missionary movement, which continues to the present time.[31] I believe that a brief analysis of the evolution of this pontifical missionary aid society is a relevant case study inasmuch as the Holy Childhood Association discloses many of the tensions and ambiguities that are inherent in efforts to understand the relationship of Christian missionary activity and Christian moral imagination.

Until the time of the Second Vatican Council, the Holy Childhood Association was best known and later caricatured for "ransoming pagan babies," promoting Lenten mite boxes, and fostering missionary vocations among impressionable children. Its secondary purpose was to lay the groundwork for commitment on the part of adult Catholics to support missionary activity through prayer and donations to the Propagation of the Faith and missionary societies.

After the Second Vatican Council, the Holy Childhood Association came under the same scrutiny as other pontifical missionary aid societies and mission associations. As tensions and divisions regarding the *missio ad gentes* intensified among church leaders, theologians, and missionaries, they trickled down to Catholic school classrooms and religious education programs. The Holy Childhood Association was identified as one of the vestiges of a pre–Vatican II ecclesiology. As changes in Roman Catholic missionary consciousness occurred in Western Europe and North America, some socially conscious, committed, and self-reflective Catholic mission educators, teachers, and catechists, affected to some degree by unexpressed guilt and moved by a desire to contribute to the process of reconciliation, readily replaced the mission education programs of the Holy Childhood Association, now considered to be obsolete, with alternative programs focused on peace and justice, world religions, human rights, and Christian values education. In many cases they effectively removed themselves from conversations on mission, evangelization, and world-church consciousness.

Some of the reasons for this were connected to an emerging, critical awareness of the shadow side of *missio ad gentes*. A few examples of such awareness included:

- awareness of the complicity of Christians in the extermination of six million Jews;
- information about poverty, racism, and oppression "at home";
- concern about anti-American and anti-European protests associated with anti-communist military interventions, multinational corporations, foreign aid/development agencies, and other forms of neocolonialism; and
- questions about the lack of "truth in advertising" with regard to the actual distribution of funds collected for designated missionary activities.

As changes in priorities and organizing principles affected missionary activity, concern for the promotion of social justice had a prophetic urgency about it that rivaled a more traditional commitment to the *missio ad gentes*, narrowly understood as involving proclamation, conversion, and catechesis. Significant differences in world views, ecclesiologies, and theologies of mission effectively contributed to the uncoupling of *missio ad gentes* and social justice, at least in the perceptions of many Catholics as well as some Protestants.

In Western Europe and North America, donations to the Holy Childhood Association began to decrease, an outward visible sign that *missio ad gentes* per se no longer captured the ecclesial imaginations of youth as it had in the past. Children in schools and parishes continued to raise funds, but they made allocations to other or at least additional groups and organizations. For thirty cents a day they were now adopting Sally Struthers's starving children instead of saving Bishop Fulton Sheen's unbaptized babies. The Lenten mite boxes of the Holy Childhood Association were replaced by the cardboard cartons of Operation Rice Bowl, the Lenten drive for Catholic Relief Services. Children, often under the influence of post–Vatican II theologies of moderate, liberal, and progressive sorts, envisioned themselves no longer as potential missionaries, but rather, as volunteers with Doctors without Borders or Habitat for Humanity. The term *missionary* was viewed by some as pejorative, precisely because of its identification with a church more interested in baptisms than the causes of infant mortality. Even missionaries themselves sought ways of distancing themselves from the nomenclature.

This shift in ecclesial consciousness had serious implications for many children in Europe and North America as well as the adults who contributed to their formation. From the perspective of social justice, they learned about racism as a social problem for the world in terms of slavery, anti-Semitism, apartheid, and genocide. However, in the absence of attention being given to the role of witness and proclamation in the *missio ad gentes*, there were few concrete ways to make the connections between racism the sin and the counter-witness of Christians to the gospel of Jesus Christ. There was no way into a dialogue about white superiority, white privilege, and cultural imperialism as structures of sin—both collective and individual.

In the early 1990s church leaders encouraged efforts to redirect the attention of Roman Catholics to the urgency of the *missio ad gentes*.[32] The 1990 papal encyclical *Redemptoris Missio* and the 1992 meeting of the Latin American Episcopal Conference (CELAM) at Santo Domingo on the new evangelization contributed to these efforts. Reacting in part to the vigorous initiatives of Protestant evangelical missionaries in Asia, Eastern Europe, and Latin America, the Vatican sought to alter the course of what had come to be described as missionary malaise in Western Europe and North America. The new impulse to mission included missionaries from around the world. Local churches in Asia, Africa, and Latin America came of age. This was signaled by their interest and desire to become missionary-sending churches. However, a question emerged: Would the initiative resolve the perceived problem, namely, the displacement of genuine zeal for the *missio ad gentes* that had been replaced by a passionate witness for justice and peace and commitments to interreligious dialogue? Or, would problems associated with *ad gentes* missionary activity be compounded?[33]

In some sectors of the world renewed zeal for proclamation tended not to be historically conscious. Memories of the tragic legacy of racism as a counter-witness to the gospel proclamation tended not to be reflected upon in any critical way. What appeared in the eyes of some to be a reassertion of a modern Western model of muscular Christianity held a certain reactionary appeal in an increasingly post-modern atmosphere influenced by the muscular relativism of the West.

And so the case study continues. As one might anticipate, a new generation of children was called upon to help support this new missionary impulse through the Holy Childhood Association. The Holy Childhood Association underwent a renaissance and a renewal.[34] Its most active members now include children from every race and many nations from around the globe. In countries like Brazil, Nigeria, the Philippines, Korea, Poland, and Mexico, these children, invited by Pope John Paul II to be ambassadors of joy, committed themselves to supporting missionaries from their own countries in bringing the message of Jesus to children in other regions of the world.

What theological meaning are we to make of renewed interest in the Holy Childhood Association? Should we presume that in the hands of missionaries from Korea, Nigeria, India, Brazil, Jamaica, Japan, Kenya, Rwanda, Guatemala, and Lithuania—and all who share a common ancestry, whether recent or distant—that the counter-witness of racism will not repeat itself, particularly in the forms of internalized racism and cross-racial hostility? Or, are we to despair at the inevitability of such a scenario? Or, should we hope that the *missio ad gentes* is, in fact, no longer defined or determined by the tragic racist legacy of the past and that this is truly a new moment for Christian mission? Based on impressionistic evidence, some seeds of hope are being sown.[35]

These questions cannot be answered yet, for they are questions that we will continue to live with for some time. These questions do, however, point to some of the concerns and anxieties related to *missio ad gentes* in the new millennium that also may be opportunities of grace and understanding. For example, what kind of moral or ecclesial imagination is informing these new and renewed missionary endeavors? What are the short-term and long-term risks involved in failure, inability, or unwillingness to recognize the ideological underpinnings of mission that contributed to the counter-witness of racism in the past and could potentially do so once again? Given the fact that the imaginations, energies, and resources of the next generation are being brought to bear on this new impulse for mission, these questions are not insignificant.

This observation brings me to the second part of my thought experiment in turning to the child. Moving from a historical case study, I would like to suggest another means of consciousness raising on the subject at hand, using the fictional portrayal of children as depicted in novels and films dealing with the *missio ad gentes*. In these two selected examples, children are the embodiment of conscience for the *missio ad gentes*. Portrayed as the most vulnerable victims of the counter-witness of racism, they also emerge as persuasive protagonists heralding the possibility of its eradication and reminding us of the paradox of mission.

Image as Insight: Children, the Conscience and Guide for the Missio ad Gentes

Whatever opinions may exist about the accuracy of portrayals of missionaries in literature and cinema, there is no denying the fact that depictions of missionary activity and attitudes about race have informed and influenced the moral imagination of those who have come under the influence of the media. From the outset, narratives and films dealing with the subject of Christian mission have held the attention of Christians and non-Christians alike. Beginning with one of the first award-winning silent films, *Missionaries in Darkest Africa* (1912), and Willa Cather's *Death Comes to the Archbishop* (1927), nine decades of novels and feature films[36] have done as much to educate for the *missio ad gentes* as a lifetime of parish mission appeals sponsored by the Propagation of the Faith, the combined volumes of nineteenth- and twentieth-century missiological research, and the collective teachings of the Christian churches on mission and missionary activity. Certainly, the fascination continues with the popularity of works such as *The Poisonwood Bible*[37] and *The Testament*.[38] Even *Star Trek: The Next Generation* counts among its episodes "Guises of the Mind,"[39] the intergalactic tale of two Poor Clare missionaries, one a peacemaker and the other a protector of abandoned orphans. Given the limits of this chapter, I have chosen to mention very briefly two examples of film segments: one from *The Mission* and one from *At Play in the Fields of the Lord.*

In the final scene of the movie *The Mission*,[40] the Mission San Carlos has been destroyed, and the Guarani Indians and the Jesuit missionaries share the same fate, death by fire and the sword. As the film concludes, a few young children make their escape from the tragic scene in a small canoe. In their faces one sees the haunting question left in the wake of the *missio ad gentes*, the recollections of all that had been and was no longer, the anxieties of an uncertain future, and the determined resiliency of a small Guarani girl, who, despite the visible disapproval of the children's leader, pulls from the river one memento of memory and hope, a floating violin of red mahogany.

At Play in the Fields of the Lord[41] is a story about contemporary missionaries and mercenaries in the Amazon rain forest. One of its central themes is cultural genocide and another is the transformation of missionary consciousness. Its child protagonists are Billy Quarrier, the young son of evangelical missionaries, and Mutu, the son of Niaruna Indians. Midway through the story Billy dies of Black River fever, surrounded by the Indians who have found in him an ambassador of joy. Once again, children are the conscience for the *missio ad gentes*, but this time we are left looking into the faces of the adult American missionaries and the adult Niaruna. Once again, we see the haunting questions left in the wake of the *missio ad gentes*, the recollection of all that had been and was no longer, the anxieties of an uncertain future, and the grief, guilt, and rage of a father, judged and found wanting by his wife, his fellow missionaries, and the Niaruna— as much a sign and symbol of contradiction as the hand-carved cross of mahogany with which he marks his son's grave.

Open to many interpretations, our moral imaginations are engaged by these children and the adult polemics of the *missio ad gentes* in which they find themselves. Surrounded by the racist counter-witness of Iberian Christian colonists in one case and the racist counter-witness of North American missionaries in the other, these fictional characters are prototypes of countless contemporary children whose faces we see on the evening news, in missionary magazines, in action alerts from Amnesty International, and in UNICEF bulletins—the refugee children of Darfur; the children trafficked in Benin; the child carpet-workers in Pakistan; the homeless children of Miami, Manila, and São Paulo; the working children of Lima; the orphaned children of Iraq; the children living and dying with AIDS in Uganda and Thailand.

Through the witness of their lives these children preach more than Christ crucified; they also proclaim the message of God-with-us. Drawing our attention not only to their otherness, but to their thisness,[42] they disclose to us the radical uniqueness that makes every child precious in God's sight. Finally, they reveal to us our own complicity in the failure to eradicate the root evil of racism in our lifetime, in the world,[43] and in the church.

As we consider the historical realities faced by these children, as well as our own historical realities, are we as theologians prepared to learn from children, to live with the questions they pose to us, to understand how the dynamics of racial privilege and all forms of racism have been and continue to influence their lives? In short, are we willing to acknowledge children as our consciences and our guides in assessing the true measure of our success as Christians in carrying out the missionary mandate of Jesus Christ in this "springtime of mission"? Will we commit ourselves to addressing, eradicating, and preventing the counter-witness that has gone on for far too long? In making a turn to the child, will we also dare to take into account exactly what attitudes and actions are being internalized by the privileged children of prestigious Catholic schools in Rio, Manila, New York, Nairobi, Tokyo, Dublin, Seoul, Mexico City, Krakow, Beirut, and Johannesburg? In posing these questions, it is my intention to blur the boundaries of the global and the local as well as those of the theological and the pastoral. To the extent that the *missio ad gentes* extends to the ends of the earth, we cannot lose sight of the fact that one need not travel to the "ends of the earth" to encounter people from the "ends of the earth" present in the urban microcosms of the world and the world church where we as theologians so often find ourselves. Wherever the racist counter-witness of Christians manifests itself, it undermines proclamation by further compounding the scandal given to some with the tacit license given to others—adults and children alike.

Looking to the Future:
An Alternative Vision and Criterion
for *Missio ad Gentes*

As Christian theologians, and more precisely as Roman Catholic theologians, we are part of an ecclesial community of confirmation and contradiction.[44] We share community with one another in the name of Jesus Christ. In the name of Jesus Christ we invite those who have not heard or understood his message to listen to our proclamation of the good news and to observe how we love one another. A holy and sinful people, we are both witnesses and counter-witnesses to the gospel we preach. Called to be missionary, we sometimes betray the trust of the very people among whom we seek to be found worthy of trust, especially the children.

Among the hard sayings of Jesus, the injunctions against those who scandalize children are unambiguous (Mk 9:42; Mt 18:6). This fact should be more than sufficient reason to do all that is in our power to remove racism as an obstacle to the *missio ad gentes*. Inasmuch as the mission of Jesus extends to the children of all races and nations, it also extends from them as well. To be receptive to a child in the name of Jesus is to receive Jesus and the One who sent him (Mk 9:37; Mt 18:5; Lk 9:48).[45] This is the hallmark of the Christian vision and criterion for receiving and entering into the reign of God: "Unless you change and become like children" (Mt 18:3–4; cf. Mk 10:15).

For many of us the world or worlds in which we live are constructed primarily by adults and for adults. It is we who benefit the most from this world, from these worlds, whether we thrive or merely survive. The farther removed we are from children who experience the consequences of racism, xenophobia, and discrimination, the less likely it is that their concerns will be or will become our own. It also might be said that the farther we are removed from missionaries and theologians whose ministries and theologies have emerged in response to the need to bind and heal these wounds, the less likely it is that their concerns will be our own.

For those of us who experience the call to articulate theologies that will serve the *missio ad gentes* in this new millennium, one way of shouldering the weight of the historical reality of racism is to begin by living with two questions: Why is the child crying? If we knew, what would we do differently?

Notes

¹ See Pope John Paul II, *Redemptoris Missio (RM)* 34 (December 12, 1990). Available at http://www.vatican.va/edocs/ENG0219/_INDEX.HTM (accessed August 23, 2006).

² The working definition for missionaries follows the description given in *Ad Gentes* IV, 23–27, and refers to those individuals and institutes in the church "who take on the duty of evangelization, which pertains to the whole Church, and make it as it were their own special task" (*AG* 23).

³ According to *RM* 36, primary obstacles to the church's missionary work include "past and present divisions among Christians, de-Christianization within Christian countries, the decrease of vocations to the apostolate, and the counter-witness of believers and Christian communities failing to follow the model of Christ in their lives."

⁴ See *RM* 58.

⁵ See Walbert Buhlmann, *Missions on Trial* (Maryknoll, NY: Orbis Books, 1979); James A. Sherer, *Missionary, Go Home! A Reappraisal of the Christian World Mission* (Englewood Cliffs, NJ: Prentice-Hall, 1964).

[6] See *RM* 35–36: "The task of proclaiming Jesus Christ to all peoples appears to be immense and out of all proportion to the Church's human resources. The difficulties seem insurmountable. . . . These difficulties [those lacking *within* the people of God] are the most painful of all [lack of fervor manifested in fatigue, disenchantment, compromise, lack of interest, and above all, lack of joy and hope]. Cf. *Evangelii Nuntiandi (EN)* 80.

[7] For example, see Stephen Bates, "Racism in Catholic Church 'Driving Minorities Away,'" *The Guardian*, October 16, 2000. Available at http://www.guardian.co.uk/race/story/0,,657380,00.html (accessed August 23, 2006).

[8] See *RM* 34: "Missionary activity proper, namely the mission *ad gentes*, is directed to 'peoples or groups who do not yet believe in Christ,' 'who are far from Christ,' in whom the Church 'has not yet taken root' (*AG* 6, 23, 27) and whose culture has not yet been influenced by the Gospel (*EN* 18–20). It is distinct from other ecclesial activities inasmuch as it is addressed to groups and settings which are non-Christian because the preaching of the Gospel and the presence of the Church are absent or insufficient."

[9] In marking the United Nations celebration of the International Day for the Elimination of Racial Discrimination, Pope John Paul II declared that "Catholics must work to ensure that no one is excluded from their communities and that people of all races and cultures feel the church is their home. . . . *It is obligatory* that religious communities join international efforts to fight racism." Available at http://www.Zenit.org, 21 March 2001 (accessed August 23, 2006).

[10] For background information, see the United Nations information site at http://www.un.org/WCAR/ (accessed August 23, 2006).

[11] Conference declarations along with post-conference statements posed numerous challenges with direct bearing on the role of religion and racism. The absence of Israel at the conference and withdrawal of the delegation from the United States highlighted conflicts in the Mideast with regard to Israel, Zionism, and the plight of the Palestinian people. Within two weeks time the tragic events of September 11 radically reframed and globalized the discourse on the religions and race in unprecedented ways. For more complete documentation on the conference, see http://www.unhchr.ch/html/racism; http://www.cnn.com/SPECIALS/2001/facing.hate/; http://www

.adl.org/durban/durban_090501.asp; and http://www.hri.ca/racism/ analyses/gshepherd.shtml (accessed August 23, 2006); Global Rights, *Next Steps for U.S. Activists: Building on Commitments Made at the United Nations World Conference against Racism* (Washington, DC: Global Rights, 2004).

[12] See The Akha Defense and Survival Project focusing on the people in Thailand's Chiangrai Province at www.Akha.org (accessed August 23, 2006).

[13] See Harvey Cox et al., "Positive Resources of Religion for Human Rights," in *Religion for Human Rights*, ed. John Kelsay and Sumner B. Twiss (New York: The Project on Religion and Human Rights, 1994), 60–79; Robert Traer, *Faith in Human Rights: Support in Religious Traditions for a Global Struggle* (Washington, DC: Georgetown University Press, 1991); and Hans Küng and Karl-Josef Kuschel, eds., *A Global Ethic: The Declaration of the Parliament of World Religions* (New York: Continuum, 1993).

[14] This definition is adapted from a compilation of resources put together by the Women's Theological Center (WTC) entitled *Racism Defined* (Boston: WTC, 1995), 2. The text here draws upon the insights of Robert W. Terry, *For Whites Only* (Grand Rapids, MI: Eerdmans, 1970); The Cornwall Collective, *Your Daughters Shall Prophesy* (New York: Pilgrim Press, 1980); bell hooks, "Overcoming White Supremacy," in *Talking Back* (Boston: South End Press, 1989); James Baldwin, *Evidence of Things Not Seen* (Cutchogue, NY: Buccaneer Books, 1995); and idem, "On Being White . . . and Other Lies," *Essence* (April 1994).

[15] WTC, *Racism Defined*, 2.

[16] Ibid.

[17] For historical background on the foundations of these statements through the mid-twentieth century, see John LaFarge, SJ, *Interracial Justice: A Study of the Catholic Doctrines of Race Relations* (1937; reprint Manchester NH: Ayer Company Publishers, 1978).

[18] Pius X, *Lacrimabili Statu: On the Indians of South America* (1912); Benedict XV, *Ad Beatissima Apostolorum: Appealing for Peace* (1914) and *Maximum Illud* (1921); Pius XI, *Rerum Ecclesiae: On the Catholic Missions* (1926) and *Mit Brennender Sorge: On the Church and the German Reich* (1937); John XXIII, *Princeps Pastorum: On the Missions, Native Clergy and Lay Participation*

(1959); Paul VI, *Populorum Progressio: On the Progress of Peoples* (1967).

[19] See the Pontifical Commission on Justice and Peace, *The Church and Racism: Towards a More Fraternal Society* (Washington, DC: U.S. Catholic Conference, 1988).

[20] Catholic Bishops of the United States, *Home Missions, Negro and Indian Missions, Foreign Missions* (1919); Catholic Bishops of the United States, *Discrimination and the Christian Conscience* (Washington, DC, 1958); Administrative Board of the National Catholic Welfare Conference, *On Racial Harmony* (Washington, DC, 1963); Catholic Bishops of the United States, *Pastoral Statement on Race Relations* (Washington, DC, 1966); Catholic Bishops of the United States, *Statement on the National Race Crisis* (Washington, DC, 1968); National Conference of Catholic Bishops, *To Do the Work of Justice* (Washington, DC: U.S. Catholic Conference, 1978); United States Catholic Bishops, *Brothers and Sisters to Us: U.S. Bishops' Pastoral Letter on Racism in Our Day* (Washington, DC: U.S. Catholic Conference, 1979); National Conference of Catholic Bishops, *The Hispanic Presence: Challenge and Commitment* (Washington, DC: U.S. Catholic Conference, 1983); Black Bishops of the United States, *What We Have Seen and Heard: A Pastoral Letter on Evangelization from the Black Bishops of the United States* (Cincinnati: St. Anthony Messenger Press, 1984); Administrative Board of the U.S. Catholic Conference, *Statement on South Africa* (Washington, DC: U.S. Catholic Conference, 1985): Administrative Board of the U.S. Catholic Conference, *Statement on the Ku Klux Klan* (Washington, DC: U.S. Catholic Conference, 1987); U.S. Catholic Conference of Bishops, "Here I Am, Send Me: A Conference Response to the Evangelization of African Americans and the National Black Catholic Pastoral Plan" (1989); National Conference of Catholic Bishops, *A Time for Remembering, Reconciling and Recommitting Ourselves as a People—Statement of the NCCB on Native Americans* (Washington, DC: U.S. Catholic Conference, 1991); U.S. Catholic Bishops, *Heritage and Hope: Evangelization in the United States* (Washington, DC: U.S. Catholic Conference, 1992); Administrative Board of the U.S. Catholic Conference, *Political Responsibility: Proclaiming the Gospel of Life, Protecting the Least among Us and Pursuing the Common Good: Reflections on the 1996 Elections* (Washington, DC: U.S. Catholic Conference, 1995).

[21] For an analysis of recent documents of individual bishops and dioceses in the United States, see Bryan N. Massingale, "James Cone and Recent Catholic Episcopal Teaching on Racism," *Theological Studies* 61, no. 4 (2000): 703.

[22] For example, speaking at the end of his weekly general audience on March 21, 2001, Pope John Paul II said that international treaties, conferences, and the upcoming World Conference on Racism are "important steps on the way toward affirming the fundamental equality and dignity of every person and for peaceful coexistence among all peoples" (available at http://zenit.org/english/, 21 March 2001 [accessed August 23, 2006]). Also, in April of 2001, commemorating the anniversary of the assassination of the Rev. Dr. Martin Luther King Jr., the Illinois Catholic bishops declared, "The springtime for the Gospel, which Pope John Paul II prays will mark the new millennium, will be a time free of racism. The time is now. Let the place be our dioceses and our state" (see "Moving beyond Racism: Learning to See with the Eyes of Christ," April 4, 2001, available at http://www.catholicnewworld.com/archive/cnw2000/0409%20/race_0409.htm [accessed on August 23, 2006]).

[23] See Eduardo Hoornaert, "Ouvi o Clamor deste Povo Negro," *Revisita Ecclesiastica Brasileira* 48, no. 189 (1988): 40–56.

[24] This notion takes as points of reference the Barmen Declaration of 1934 of the Lutheran Churches in Germany and the Belmar Declaration of 1981 of the Dutch Reformed Churches in South Africa.

[25] Among others, I would include John LaFarge, Yves Conger, Austin Flannery, Thomas Merton, Rosemary Radford Ruether, Anne Patrick, Walbert Buhlmann, Daniel Berrigan, Johannes B. Metz, and Albert Nolan.

[26] Sharon Parks, *The Critical Years* (New York: Harper and Row, 1986), 116.

[27] See David Bosch, *Transforming Mission* (Maryknoll, NY: Orbis Books, 1992).

[28] These observations are adapted from Parks, *The Critical Years*, 117.

[29] See Stephen B. Bevans and Roger P. Schroeder, *Constants in Context: A Theology of Mission for Today* (Maryknoll, NY: Orbis Books, 2004).

[30] See *RM* 2, 86.

[31] See Charles Dollen, *Charity without Frontiers* (Collegeville, MN: Liturgical Press, 1972), 34–35. The Holy Childhood Association came under the direction and administration of the Propagation of the Faith and eventually was given the status of a pontifical mission aid society.

[32] See William R. Burrows, ed., *Redemption and Dialogue: Reading* Redemptoris Missio *and* Dialogue and Proclamation (Maryknoll, NY: Orbis Books, 1993).

[33] Examples of such problems included the lack of sufficient cross-cultural training of missionaries, difficulties in ecumenical relations with Protestant missionaries and Orthodox church leaders, problems with religious extremism, the threat of reprisals and persecutions, identification of missionaries with right-wing political movements, a recapitulation of the counter-witness for which missionaries had been criticized in the past, and so forth.

[34] See summary of Annual Report 2001–2002 by Rev. Patrick Byrne, SVD, Secretary General. Available at http://www.fides.org/spa/congregazione/poim_2002.html (accessed August 23, 2006).

[35] An example of such hope is described by Marianne Farina, CSC: "In Bangladesh, we face the issue of racism and prejudice between various groups in Bangladesh. Therefore, racism and prejudice are at the heart of the Church's ecclesiological reflection. As part of the Church's efforts to heal and recover an authentic voice proclaiming the Gospel, the Holy Childhood Association in Bangladesh promotes the reality that every child in Bangladesh, be he or she Christian, Muslim, Hindu, Buddhist or Animist, be he or she Bengali, Shantal, Mandi or Oran, he or she is a *Holy Child of God*. It has been a very positive program and during my eleven years there, I saw great changes occur through these reflections."

[36] For a more complete analysis, see Alan Neely, "Images: Mission and Missionaries in Contemporary Fiction and Cinema," *Missiology* 24, no. 4 (1996): 451–78. (This includes a complete listing of novels and films through 1995.)

[37] Barbara Kingsolver, *The Poisonwood Bible* (New York: HarperCollins, 1998).

[38] John Grisham, *The Testament* (New York: Doubleday, 1999).

[39] Rebecca Neason, "Guises of the Mind," *Star Trek: The Next Generation*, no. 27 (1993).

[40] Robert Bolt (screenwriter), *The Mission*, directed by Roland Joffé (1986).

[41] Peter Matthieson, *At Play in the Field of the Lord* (New York: Vintage Books, 1991 [1965]). Directed by Hector Babenco (1991).

[42] For further discussion of the Scotist notion of "thisness" *(haecceitas)*, see Mary Beth Ingham, CSJ, "The Harmony of Goodness: Mutuality as a Context for Scotus' Moral Framework," in *The Ethical Method of John Duns Scotus: A Contribution to Roman Catholic Moral Theology*, ed. Thomas A. Shannon and Mary Beth Ingham (St. Bonaventure, NY: Franciscan Institute, 1992); and *Spirit and Life: A Journal of Contemporary Franciscanism* 3 (1993): 63.

[43] This was the envisioned future set out by the General Assembly of the United Nations Declaration on the Elimination of All Forms of Racial Discrimination on November 20, 1963. See Resolution 1904 (xviii).

[44] Parks, *The Critical Years*, 129.

[45] The statement parallels the reward of discipleship as described in Matthew, "Whoever welcomes you welcomes me, and whoever welcomes me welcomes the one who sent me" (Mt 10:40), and in John, "Very truly, I tell you, whoever receives one whom I send receives me; and whoever receives me receives him who sent me" (Jn 13:20).

PART III

CONSTRUCTIVE THEOLOGICAL INTERRUPTIONS OF WHITE PRIVILEGE

7

• • • •

THE TRANSFORMATIVE POWER
OF THE PERIPHERY

Can a White U.S. Catholic Opt for the Poor?

Margaret R. Pfeil

When Laurie Cassidy and Alex Mikulich invited me to present a paper in the White Privilege Developing Group at the 2003 annual meeting of the Catholic Theological Society of America, I considered the issue of whiteness through the theological lens of the option for the poor. Now, three years later, my own self-understanding as a white U.S. Catholic having been further awakened, I will offer here a theological and ethical account of the implications of white privilege that reflects the fruit of my continuing journey, which I hope is one of conversion. It may be possible for a white U.S. Catholic to opt for the poor, but not without personal accountability as a beneficiary of white privilege and an ongoing commitment to subvert the power structures of white supremacy both within the church and in society.

Before considering how institutionalized white privilege might be disrupted through the transformative power available at the societal margins, I will explore the meaning of whiteness. I do so advisedly, aware that by giving sustained attention to whiteness, I may inadvertently reinforce its dominance. But, precisely because white privilege typically goes unchallenged, above all by white people, interrogating whiteness is a necessary step in identifying and then dismantling structures of white supremacy through the solidarity of Christian love. Along the way I will use American studies scholar Ruth Frankenberg's compelling analysis of whiteness to illuminate its insidious effects within U.S. society and the U.S. Catholic Church.

The Option for the Poor

White privilege, in general terms, functions systemically, invisibly, and without name while at the same time conferring power.[1] Originally, I used the option for the poor to examine the structural dynamics of white privilege because in the work of liberation theology it has provided a valuable perspective from which to analyze institutionalized violence, systemic oppression, and societal power disparities. To opt for the poor represents a constitutive dimension of Christian discipleship, as the U.S. bishops articulated in their 1986 pastoral letter, *Economic Justice for All*:

> From the Scriptures and church teaching, we learn that the justice of a society is tested by the treatment of the poor. The justice that was the sign of God's covenant with Israel was measured by how the poor and unprotected . . . were treated. The kingdom that Jesus proclaimed in his word and ministry excludes no one. . . . As followers of Christ, we are challenged to make a fundamental "option for the poor"—to speak for the voiceless, to defend the defenseless, to assess life styles, policies, and social institutions in terms of their impact on the poor.[2]

But those marginalized by institutionalized oppression are neither voiceless nor powerless. Rather, their voices go unheeded, and their exercises of power meet with crushing, violent resistance reinforced by structures of domination. Taking this reality into account, those who opt for the poor must position themselves to listen to and accompany those human beings relegated to the margins of society by various and variable structures of exploitation. From this vantage point one is better able to give concrete expression to solidarity, what John Paul II described in *Sollicitudo Rei Socialis* as "a commitment to the good of one's neighbor with the readiness, in the gospel sense, to 'lose oneself' for the sake of the other instead of exploiting him, and to 'serve him' instead of oppressing him for one's own advantage (cf. Matt. 10:40–42; 20:25; Mark 10:42–45; Luke 22:25–27)."[3]

What does it really mean for me "to lose myself" as a white U.S. Catholic? Three years ago I asserted that in opting to stand on the ecclesial and societal margins, the Christian disciple must attend, above all, to the voices of those oppressed by structures of white privilege, for these are arguably the most oppressed both within the U.S. Catholic Church and in U.S. society. What I have learned since then and continue to understand more deeply is the extent to which I as a white U.S. Catholic have been morally crippled by my formation and complicity in white privilege. In order to opt for the poor I need to name my own formidable blindness to the structures of white supremacy from which I have benefited throughout my life. My race-based unearned advantages have conferred a certain kind of power, one that springs from the destructive force of domination rather than from the generative solidarity of Christian love. Left unexamined and unchallenged, my whiteness continues to function as a form of social violence and therefore renders me incapable of truly opting for the poor. When a group of people, James Baldwin writes, "are able to persuade themselves that another group or breed of men are less than men, they themselves become less than men and have made it almost impossible for themselves to confront reality and to change it."[4] Absent radical conversion, I as a white person will remain paralyzed in silent, dehumanizing complicity.

I still find that the option for the poor provides a useful theological departure point for white U.S. Catholics to begin to name our participation in structures of white privilege and to undertake the transformative action of solidarity. But I see now that while these acts of love might serve the end of justice for all people of color harmed by white privilege, they also represent the path of Christian salvation for white people. Because it requires that we confront the systemic implications of our whiteness, the option for the poor offers white U.S. Catholics a glimmer of hope that we might, by grace, be set free from the terrible trap that Baldwin described, freed to take responsibility for our whiteness by subverting structures of white privilege.

Whiteness and "Standpoint Epistemology"

Theologically, the option for the poor takes root in relationship with the God of life in faith and involves two dimensions, one epistemological and the other activist.[5] One who opts to stand on the societal margins with those excluded assumes an interpretive standpoint that yields data not readily available at the center of dominant social power. Adopting the epistemological departure point of the periphery leads one, by grace, to affirm, defend, and nurture the lives of all human beings, especially the most vulnerable.

As Ruth Frankenberg points out, whiteness also constitutes a standpoint from which one views oneself and social reality. Epistemologically, whiteness involves the construction of knowledge claims from a social location of dominance. Confronting this reality, James Cone took white Catholic theologians to task for a sort of race-based epistemological arrogance, charging in *Theological Studies*, "I have yet to read a White Catholic theologian who regarded Black history and culture as essential to their articulation of the faith. . . . If one read only White Catholic theologians, one would hardly know that Blacks exist in America or had the capacity for thought about God. White theological reflections are limited to their own culture and history as if they are the only thinkers on the planet."[6]

Such intellectual impoverishment is symptomatic of the epistemological plight of dominant social locations, according to Sandra Harding. Insofar as the privileges conferred by the standpoint of whiteness escape critical scrutiny by those who are white, the social location of whiteness can be considered epistemologically compromised.[7] This blindness represents a severe moral handicap for whites because, as Karin Case notes, "the system of white supremacy limits our consciousness, restricts our vision, and structures social relations so that all too frequently we remain silent and inert in the face of injustice."[8]

Even given these significant intellectual and moral liabilities of white supremacy, though, white people typically cling tightly to our dominant epistemological standpoint, and, in fact, we are often socialized to be oblivious to it. "Whites have difficulty perceiving whiteness," Martha Mahoney writes, "both because of its cultural prevalence and because of its cultural dominance. . . . Like culture, race is something whites notice in themselves only in relation to others. Privileged identity requires reinforcement and maintenance, but protection against seeing the mechanisms that socially reproduce and maintain privilege is an important component of the privilege itself."[9] Remaining blind to the social, political, economic, and cultural implications of whiteness constitutes a pyrrhic prerogative of whiteness, an insidious symptom of dominance that dehumanizes every member of society.

In the past I indicated that while whites may profess our blindness, whiteness and its oppressive privileges are all too visible to those who are dehumanized by them. I now recognize that in so stating the case, I neglected the painfully obvious truth that white beneficiaries of race-based advantages contribute to the destruction of our own humanity precisely by silently accepting such privilege, and that is a choice we make as moral agents. To opt for the poor as a white U.S. Catholic, then, entails consciously choosing a radically different standpoint that will allow critical questions about white privilege to emerge.[10] More than a mere shift in viewpoint, this epistemological dimension of the option for the poor opens the way toward moral, intellectual, and spiritual conversion.

Ocular Epistemology and the Social Construction of Whiteness

An important aspect of this *metanoia* involves a critical analysis of the construction of knowledge claims that support structures of white privilege. Of particular concern is what Shawn Copeland has insightfully identified as the "ocular epistemological illusion" that equates knowing with simply looking at that which is visible: "Such a foundation for knowing is easily seduced to support the Eurocentric aesthetic 'normative gaze' with its attendant racist, sexist, imperialist, and pornographic connotations."[11]

Ocular epistemological illusion, for example, played a part in Enlightenment attempts to categorize human beings according to "objective" measures of race.[12] In the late eighteenth century, German professor of medicine Johann Blumenbach assigned the name Caucasian to European whites because he found them to be the most attractive of the various groupings of humanity that he studied. "He felt that the women of the Caucasus region in Russia were the most beautiful of all Europeans. Value judgments about other human groups varied insofar as they departed from this ideal."[13] Blumenbach's ocular epistemology thus helped to establish the normativity of whiteness as an "objective" criterion of measurement. Once articulated, standards tend to escape scrutiny. The measure recedes into the background as attention becomes focused upon the objects to be compared to the norm, now taken for granted. Viewed through the lens of ocular epistemology, the standard of whiteness becomes "invisible" and its objective normativity assumed.

Ocular epistemology contributes to the social construction of whiteness as a historically conditioned and relational category. "Like other racial locations," Frankenberg writes, "it has no inherent but only socially constructed meanings."[14] In the 1806 case of *Hudgins v. Wright*, for example, "three generations of enslaved women sued for freedom in Virginia on the ground that they descended from a free maternal ancestor." The case turned on the judge's interpretation of the women's visible bodily traits. "The youngest . . . [had] the characteristic features, the complexion, the hair and eyes . . . the same with those of whites. . . . Hannah [the mother] had long black hair, was of the right Indian copper colour, and was generally called an Indian by the neighbors."[15] Judge Tucker ruled that these physiological markers were sufficient proof of the women's claim of descent from an Indian (free) woman. "Nature has stamped upon the African and his descendants two characteristic marks, besides the difference of complexion, which often remain visible long after the characteristic distinction of colour either disappears or becomes doubtful; a flat nose and a woolly head of hair."[16]

While the meaning of whiteness and other racial categories may be viewed as social constructions, the historically conditioned interpretation of their meaning carries very real and dehumanizing consequences. In Virginia in 1806 the physical features of the Wright women, subjected to the scrutiny of the ocular epistemological lens according to the uncontested norm of whiteness, determined the difference between freedom and enslavement.

What was initially less apparent to me as a white interpreter of this narrative, but no less real, is the extent to which Judge

Tucker, the appointed arbiter of white privilege in this case, ultimately forfeited his human dignity in the process. Reflecting the conventional, encoded white wisdom of his time, he was vested with the social power to arbitrate the liberty of other human beings but was tragically blind to his own interior binds safely secured by the white supremacist legal and political structures that placed the onus of such a dehumanizing task upon him. Presumably, though, he was not coerced into playing that role. With some degree of freedom as a moral agent, he chose to cooperate with an objectively sinful system.

Whiteness as a Social Location of Race-based Structural Advantage

That those occupying the epistemological standpoint of white supremacy fall prey to moral blindness does not mean that whiteness is invisible. Rather, invisibility is a feature of the powerful matrices of privilege that accompany it. Whiteness, Frankenberg argues, represents "a location of structural advantage in societies structured in racial dominance."[17] Thomas Wyatt Turner, the founder of the Federation of Colored Catholics, witnessed the painful reality of institutionalized white supremacy incarnated in the U.S. Catholic Church. In October 1919 he wrote to E. R. Dyer, the president of St. Mary's Seminary in Baltimore, to ask if he would reject prospective candidates who were identifiably black. Rev. Dyer responded:

> We could not admit colored students as members of our Seminary Community because this would make it impossible for us to serve a great many Bishops and dioceses who now depend upon us for the education of their clergy and who would be unwilling to commit their subjects to us if we received colored students.[18]

The structural effects of white privilege upon the catholicity of the church were not lost on Turner and the Federation of Colored Catholics. In 1926 they noted in their first letter to the U.S. Catholic bishops that while forty-two black priests served the continent of Africa, there were only five in the United States.[19] In response to Dyer, Turner rightly noted the sinful complicity of white priests and laity in maintaining ecclesial structures of white supremacy:

> The Catholic colored people have tied themselves, in the Church, up to the Banner of the Lord Jesus Christ, which we think we recognize quite clearly; but when a white majority, in the Church, shall for social purposes abandon this Banner we shall certainly not be misled. If all the white priests and laymen decide that segregating and discriminating Catholics are reasonable in the Catholic church we shall still cling to the undefiled Banner of the Lord even though we may have to tread the "wine press alone."[20]

Turner poignantly named the reality that his white interlocutors failed to perceive: Their location of structural advantage as white Catholics, defended through the dehumanizing power of white supremacy, made a mockery of their profession of faith as disciples of Jesus Christ. Whites who acquiesced to these ecclesial structures of white dominance essentially put themselves outside the church.

Lamentably, Turner's prophetic indictment remains salient in the U.S. Catholic Church of the twenty-first century. Black Catholics convened the first lay congress in the United States in 1889,[21] yet in spite of such exemplary ministerial leadership, they continue to experience racial discrimination as a "minority within a minority" in the Catholic church.[22] As the African American bishops decried in their pastoral letter on evangelization, African Americans are still relegated to the margins of ecclesial life,[23] and whites continue to occupy the dominant center of ecclesial power structures. In his 2001 pastoral letter on racism Cardinal George was able to quote the U.S. bishops' 1979 document *Brothers and Sisters to Us*. Unfortunately, it still applies in 2006: "All too often in the very places where blacks, Hispanics, Native Americans, and Asians are numerous, the Church's officials and representatives, both clerical and lay, are predominantly white."[24] Thus, even as the U.S. Catholic Church becomes more racially and ethnically diverse, with Latinos/as now making up 44 percent of the U.S. Catholic population under the age of ten,[25] the sin of institutionalized white racial dominance continues to impede its evangelizing mission.

The U.S. Catholic Church continues to struggle to balance "racial particularity and religious universality,"[26] and one reason may be found in its narrative. The racial particularity of the U.S. Catholic Church has storied roots, exemplifying Frankenberg's observation that inclusion in the white racial category varies in relation to historically conditioned interpretations of race and ethnicity. As John McGreevy has indicated, Catholic immigrants to the United States in the late nineteenth and early twentieth centuries encountered a racialized context that distinguished Celtic, Polish, German, Italian, and Anglo-Saxon "races" but was nonetheless dominated by the black/white racial binary. Gradually, Euro-Americans claimed a common identity as white, with each ethnic group assiduously seeking to avoid any taint of the racial inferiority associated with blacks.[27] As some urban immigrant parishes began to merge across ethnic lines by the 1930s, segregation of black Catholics became all the more conspicuous as a sign of white Catholic racism. W. E. B. Du Bois aptly named the church's betrayal of its mission through its complicity in white supremacy: "Because Catholicism has so much that is splendid in its past . . . it is the greater shame that 'nigger' haters clothed in its episcopal robes should do to black Americans in exclusion [and] segregation . . . all that the Ku Klux Klan ever asked."[28]

At the risk of reinforcing the black/white racial binary, I have chosen to attend mainly to the marginalization of black Catholics in this essay in light of this historical process by which white U.S. Catholics of many ethnic backgrounds constructed the protocols of white supremacy, establishing the blackness of African Americans as the antithesis of whiteness. The same logic positing the superiority of whiteness as the normative standard has been applied to other racial and ethnic groups not identified as white in the U.S. Catholic Church and in U.S. society, and current examples abound, the highly racialized national debate about immigration reform being one of them.

Whiteness in Relation to Other Measures of Power

Understanding whiteness as a historically conditioned and socially constructed category engenders appreciation of the ways that it confers privilege variably in relation to other indices of social power. White race privilege, Frankenberg notes, takes shape in fluid interaction with "other axes of relative advantage or sub-ordination; these do not erase or render irrelevant race privilege, but rather inflect or modify it."[29] Race, for example, is a stronger predictor than class for the location of toxic waste dumps in the United States, but historically both factors have intersected as components of environmental racism.[30] Communities that would now be identified as white have been environmentally mar-ginalized in the past, Sylvia Hood Washington writes, because "they were either considered not white or not part of the main-stream white community."[31] The geographical circumscription and toxic pollution of Chicago's Back of the Yards neighborhoods in the late nineteenth and early twentieth centuries represented institutionalized policies designed to protect "native white" com-munities at the expense of the more recently arrived European immigrants who lived there.[32]

To take another example, people of color, and African Ameri-cans in particular, are disproportionately represented on death row in the United States.[33] The chances of a poor white male being sentenced to death are higher than for a white male of greater economic means but still less than for a black male. White racial privilege remains operative, but it is inflected by class in this con-text.

Along the axis of gender Traci West notes that even prior to the events of 9/11, the U.S. General Accounting Office "reported that for fiscal year 1997 black women U.S. citizens were more likely to be strip-searched at airports by U.S. customs agents than white men and women, Asian men and women, and Hispanic men and women passengers, regardless of whether they were U.S. citizens," and the group second-most-likely to undergo strip searches were black women who were non-U.S. citizens.[34] In this case being black and female proved a stronger predictor than citizenship in determining the risk of being strip-searched, and if anything, citizenship seems to have worked against U.S. black women.

Like other U.S. white women, I might readily identify with the sexual discrimination and bodily degradation exhibited in this example, but it is more difficult for me to perceive that these statistics confirm the relative exemption of white women from such subjugation. As Peggy McIntosh has emphasized, white privi-lege is operative when I lament the unjust treatment of people of color without also acknowledging my own race-based immunity from that experience. "How terrible for you" finds its typically unspoken correlate in "How exempt for me."[35]

Dismantling Structures of White Privilege

How might the option for the poor open ground for dismantling structures of white privilege? In the U.S. Catholic ecclesial context, Turner, Du Bois, and Cone point toward the need to retrieve and celebrate tradition in a manner that accounts for the voices and the power of black Catholics. One of the many gifts that black Catholics have bestowed upon the U.S. Catholic Church, Diana Hayes notes, is the exercise of critical mediation in the form of "'subversive memory' within the church itself. Black Catholics call the church to live up to its proclamation of scriptures that reveal God's consistent option for the poor and the oppressed, scriptures that have been too often submerged by a praxis that ignored the plight of those same poor and oppressed."[36]

Subversive memory invites white U.S. Catholics to follow the witness of Christian discipleship given by enslaved Africans. To them, Shawn Copeland notes, Jesus meant freedom. "To understand the fearless and dangerous Jesus was to break the spell cast by the prevailing dominative consciousness—to break with a slave mentality. To understand the fearless and dangerous Jesus was to release the Word of God from the grip of the slave holders and set it free working in the midst of those yearning to be free."[37]

Gripped by the structures of white privilege to which we have given at least tacit assent by virtue of our uncontested and bloody accrual of advantage from them, white U.S. Catholics may perhaps find in Jesus' peripheral stance our own distinctive invitation to freedom. Subverting societal structures of white privilege represents the key to unlocking the shackles of our own making. For most white U.S. Catholics, this sort of liberation will mean relinquishing a violently dominant form of power and following Jesus to the societal periphery, there to learn from him a different potency.

Working from the margins of his own society, Jesus used his power to resist structures of sin. Rosita deAnn Mathews astutely observes that Jesus "took a peripheral posture to the establishment. He did not sell his soul or give his allegiance to them. . . .

By remaining on the periphery of the system, he was able to utilize his power to change the system and not perpetuate it."[38] The
vantage point of the margins, Jesus demonstrated, makes available the blocked energy of an alternative form of power. Rejecting the destructive path of violent domination, he tapped into the
power of solidarity, taking advantage of what systems theorists
call synergy.

This kind of "power-with," explains Joanna Macy, "is not a
property one can own, but a process one engages in."[39] By contrast to possessive domination, synergy thrives on open channels
of communication in which all participants contribute to the health
of the whole by allowing creative energy to flow freely through
them in service of the common good. Closing off those lines of
generative participation comes at a steep price. Even when those
wielding dominant power appear to emerge with the material
goods that serve as the talismanic symbols of success in Western
cultures, in truth all of God's creation suffers. "Take the neuron
in the neural net," Macy suggests. "If it were, hypothetically, to
suppose that its powers were a personal property to be preserved
and protected from other nerve cells, and isolated itself behind
defensive walls, it would atrophy, or die. Its health and its power
lie in opening itself to the charge, letting the signals through.
Only then can the larger systems of which it is a part learn to
respond and think."[40]

Synergistic power resides in the dynamic emergence of new
creative possibilities that only come to fruition through the coop-
eration of all the parts of a living system in behalf of the whole.
Together they share a vibrant life force that no one of them could
access apart from the rest. This form of power resonates with the
Spirit-driven variety that Jesus invited his disciples to cultivate,
and it seems to coincide with John Paul II's vision of solidarity as
a virtue: It is "not a feeling of vague compassion or shallow dis-
tress at the misfortunes of so many people, both near and far. On
the contrary, it is *a firm and persevering determination* to commit oneself to the *common good*; that is to say to the good of all
and of each individual, because we are *all* really responsible *for
all*" (emphasis in original).[41]

Building on scriptural evidence, the Christian tradition has
consistently upheld the option for the poor as a means of
enfleshing solidarity in service of the common good. Catholic

social-teaching texts have often invoked the option for the poor in relation to matters of distributive justice, generally emphasizing the universal destination of created goods as a fundamental principle. Thus, Paul VI affirmed in *Populorum Progressio:* "It is well-known how strong were the words used by the Fathers of the Church to describe the proper attitude of persons who possess anything toward persons in need. To quote Saint Ambrose: 'You are not making a gift of your possessions to the poor person. You are handing over to him what is his. For what has been given in common for the use of all, you have arrogated to yourself. The world is given to all, and not only to the rich.'"[42]

And, the world is given to all, not only to white people. In relation to the task of dismantling white privilege, the option for the poor entails grappling with the lasting effects of what has been called the original American sin, the enslavement of Africans as personal possessions rendered possible by a stunning assumption of white entitlement. The legacy of this systematic and violent commodification of black human beings bears with it a particular form of social concupiscence, one that predisposes U.S. Americans to fall prey to the seductive promises of a consumerist culture. Rapid accumulation of material wealth, the overarching *telos* that drove the slave economy, continues to take priority over the lives of those deemed expendable on a global scale, and particularly of those who are not perceived as white. The current prevalence of armed vigilante groups on the U.S.-Mexico border, ostensibly to protect private property, illustrates the prioritization of material possessions over human life not identifiably white.

As Dorothee Soelle noted in *The Silent Cry*, violence is often deployed in defense of material goods, buttressed by a fortress of ego. In the white-knuckled grip of possessions, one comes finally to the point of being completely possessed by them, ultimately forfeiting one's very identity to them. Dante's moneylenders come to mind here, absorbed forever on the outer reaches of the seventh circle of hell by loveless fascination with the moneybags strung around their necks.[43] For them, consummate absorption in material things meant the final consumption of their humanity. They commodified their very selves. In the end, they found not egolessness but the implosion of personal identity, rendering them incapable of self-giving in relationship to God and other human beings.

On the other hand, as Soelle notices, "Becoming empty or 'letting go' of the ego, possession, and violence is the precondition of the creativity of transforming action."[44] This graced path of surrender invites those occupying positions of social dominance, and white U.S. Americans above all, to renounce their violent power in favor of the potency of solidarity on the periphery of society. With the most to lose materially and the greatest leverage to prevent such loss, beneficiaries of interlocking forms of privilege, and particularly of white supremacy, face the acute spiritual challenge of letting go of that which captivates and holds all captive in the despair of what Cornel West calls lives of "'random nows,' of fortuitous and fleeting moments preoccupied with . . . acquiring pleasure, property, and power by any means necessary."[45]

Those enjoying dominance at the intersection of race, gender, and class may find freedom from enslavement to possession, including attachment to privilege, through the graced discipline of asceticism. For white U.S. Americans this contemplative commitment to simplicity will involve both material and spiritual elements. In James Perkinson's sobering assessment, most whites will find that "antiracist conversion implies at least some form of real material contraction expressed as a form of social expansion. It implies pursuing a more equal circulation of assets, opportunities, and power that will simultaneously be experienced as a form of real loss. . . . In a finite world, expanded forms of solidarity and political community cannot be birthed without real loss in relationship to the status quo and serious negotiation of that loss."[46] As Noel Ignatiev and John Garvey have asserted, whites essentially must become "race traitors," resisting institutionalized racism by challenging white supremacist practices and assumptions in the structuring of determinative indices of the common good like education, housing, hiring policies, and environmental health.[47] An important piece of this effort entails the ongoing conscientization of other whites regarding the destructive social power that we accrue through institutionalized white entitlement.[48]

The graced ability to renounce the material binds of white racial dominance will need to take root in God's love through spiritual *askesis*. White people have to face the painful task of simultaneously resisting the sinfulness that white racial identity enacts while also discovering anew through transformative acts of racial solidarity the truth of God's love for all human beings, even white people. This is no small feat. Referring to an exercise commonly used in race-relations work, Jennifer Harvey offers a glimpse of the formidable challenge facing whites: "If you were to ask a group of white people to make a list of five characteristics unique to our racial identity that do not result from power and privilege, we, unlike our sisters and brothers of colors, will have little or nothing to offer."[49] Developing a non-oppressive white racial identity will require the spiritual practices of the desert, particularly true contrition and the humility born of radical surrender. Through grace, contemplative dwelling in God's love may provide white people with the strength needed to subvert the power structures of white supremacy.

By following Jesus to the societal and ecclesial margins and there engaging the power of Christian love, it may be possible for white U.S. Catholics truly to opt for the poor. At a time when Roman Catholics constitute 23 percent of the U.S. population, the church is poised to effect transformative social change by witnessing to racial solidarity as an essential part of its mission. But, this will only be possible if U.S. Catholics, and whites in particular, cleanse the church of institutionalized racism, beginning with entrenched structures of white privilege. For white U.S. Catholics opting for the poor means, above all, accepting Jesus' invitation to radical freedom, exchanging the violent power of racial domination for the power of solidarity on the periphery.

Notes

[1] See Stephanie M. Wildman, *Privilege Revealed: How Invisible Preference Undermines America* (New York: New York University Press, 1996).

[2] *Economic Justice for All*, 16, in *Catholic Social Thought: The Documentary Heritage*, ed. David J. O'Brien and Thomas A. Shannon (Maryknoll, NY: Orbis Books, 1992), 574–75.

[3] John Paul II, *Sollicitudo Rei Socialis*, 38, in O'Brien and Shannon, *Catholic Social Thought*, 422.

[4] James Baldwin, "White Racism or World Community?" in *The Price of the Ticket: Collected Nonfiction 1948–1985* (New York: St.

Martin's/Marek, 1985), 440. This essay originally appeared in *Ecumenical Review* (October 1968).

⁵ See Gregory Baum, "Option for the Powerless," *The Ecumenist* (November-December 1987): 80–86.

⁶ James H. Cone, "Black Liberation Theology and Black Catholics: A Critical Conversation," *Theological Studies* 61 (2000): 741.

⁷ Sandra Harding, "Rethinking Standpoint Epistemology: What Is 'Strong Objectivity'?" in *Feminist Epistemologies*, ed. Linda Alcoff and Elizabeth Potter (New York: Routledge, 1993), 54.

⁸ Karin A. Case, "Claiming White Social Location as a Site of Resistance to White Supremacy," in *Disrupting White Supremacy from Within: What White People Need to Do*, ed. Jennifer Harvey, Karin A. Case, and Robin Hawley Gorsline (Cleveland, OH: Pilgrim Press, 1994), 65.

⁹ Martha R. Mahoney, "The Social Construction of Whiteness," in *Critical White Studies: Looking behind the Mirror*, ed. Richard Delgado and Jean Stefancic (Philadelphia: Temple University Press, 1997), 331. In the same volume, see also Peggy McIntosh, "White Privilege and Male Privilege: A Personal Account of Coming to See Correspondences through Work in Women's Studies," 293–94.

¹⁰ Harding, "Rethinking Standpoint Epistemology," 56.

¹¹ M. Shawn Copeland, "Foundations for Catholic Theology in an African American Context," in *Black and Catholic: The Challenge and Gift of Black Folk*, ed. Jamie T. Phelps (Milwaukee: Marquette University Press, 1997), 112. Copeland points to Cornel West's *Prophesy Deliverance! An Afro-American Revolutionary Christianity* (Philadelphia: Westminster Press, 1982), 47–65, and Susan Griffin's "Pornography and Silence," in *Made from This Earth: An Anthology of Writings by Susan Griffin* (New York: Harper and Row, 1982), 110–60. She makes the same point in "The Exercise of Black Theology in the United States," *Journal of Hispanic/Latino Theology* 3, no. 3 (1996): 11. See also Clarence Rufus J. Rivers, "The Oral African Tradition versus the Ocular Western Tradition: The Spirit of Worship," in *Taking Down Our Harps: Black Catholics in the United States*, ed. Diana L. Hayes and Cyprian Davis (Maryknoll, NY: Orbis Books, 1998), 239. Rivers notes that Aristotle begins *Metaphysics* with the exhortation, "Of all the senses, trust only the sense of sight." Thich Nhat Hanh, reflecting a Buddhist perspective, also notes the epistemological limits of seeing: What one is able to see and understand is a function of who one has become as

a person. "There are those who look into the eyes of the Buddha, into the eyes of Jesus, but who are not capable of seeing the Buddha or Jesus" (Thich Nhat Hanh and Daniel Berrigan, *The Raft Is Not the Shore* [1975; reprint Maryknoll, NY: Orbis Books, 2001], 113).

[12] See Audrey Smedley, *Race in North America: Origin and Evolution of a Worldview* (Boulder, CO: Westview Press, 1994), 150–68. See also Richard Delgado, *The Rodrigo Chronicles: Conversations about America and Race* (New York: New York University Press, 1995), 158.

[13] Smedley, *Race in North America*, 164.

[14] Ruth Frankenberg, "The Mirage of an Unmarked Whiteness," in *The Making and Unmaking of Whiteness*, ed. Birgit Brander Rasmussen et al. (Durham, NC: Duke University Press, 2001), 76.

[15] Ian F. Haney Lopez, "The Social Construction of Race," in *Critical Race Theory: The Cutting Edge*, ed. Richard Delgado and Jean Stefancic (Philadelphia: Temple University Press, 2000), 163, quoting from *Hudgins v. Wright*, 11 Va. 134 (1 Hen. & M.) (Sup. Ct. App. 1806).

[16] Haney Lopez, "The Social Construction of Race," 163–64, quoting from *Hudgins v. Wright*, 139–40.

[17] Frankenberg, "The Mirage of an Unmarked Whiteness," 76.

[18] Marilyn W. Nickels, "Thomas Wyatt Turner and the Federated Colored Catholics," *U.S. Catholic Historian* 7, nos. 2 and 3 (1988): 222–23, quoting from "Dyer to Turner, 14 October 1919," Turner Papers, Moorland-Spingarn Research Center, Howard University, Washington, D.C. (unpublished memoirs).

[19] Nickels, "Thomas Wyatt Turner and the Federated Colored Catholics," 227, citing "Federated Colored Catholics to the American bishops, November 1926," Turner Papers. Cyprian Davis cites one estimate that there were about 200,000 black Catholics in the United States in 1920 (*The History of Black Catholics in the United States* [New York: Crossroad, 1995], 231).

[20] Nickels, "Thomas Wyatt Turner and the Federated Colored Catholics," 223, quoting "Turner to Dyer, 18 October 1919," Turner Papers.

[21] Cyprian Davis, O.S.B., "Black Catholics in Nineteenth-Century America," *U.S. Catholic Historian* 5, no. 1 (1986): 14–15.

[22] Albert J. Raboteau, "Black Catholics and Afro-American Religious History: Autobiographic Reflections," *U.S. Catholic Historian* 5, no. 1 (1986): 124.

[23] Joseph Howze et al., *What We Have Seen and Heard: Essays and Stories from Black Catholics of Baltimore* (Cincinnati: St. Anthony Messenger Press, 1984), 20.

[24] U.S. Catholic Bishops, *Brothers and Sisters to Us* (Washington: National Conference of Catholic Bishops, 1979), 4; Francis Cardinal George, *Dwell in My Love* (Chicago: Archdiocese of Chicago, 2001), 11.

[25] U.S. Conference of Catholic Bishops, *Catholic Information Project* (Washington: USCCB, 2006), 4.

[26] Raboteau, "Black Catholics and Afro-American Religious History," 124.

[27] John T. McGreevy, *Parish Boundaries: The Catholic Encounter with Race in the Twentieth Century Urban North* (Chicago: University of Chicago Press, 1996), 34. See also James R. Barrett and David Roediger, "How White People Became White," in Delgado and Stefancic, *Critical White Studies*, 403. On the problematic aspects of the black/white binary, see Juan F. Perea, "The Black/White Binary Paradigm of Race," in Delgado and Stefancic, *Critical Race Theory*, 344–53.

[28] W. E. B. Du Bois, "The Catholic Church and Negroes," *The Crisis* 30 (July 1925): 121, cited in McGreevy, *Parish Boundaries*, 35.

[29] Frankenberg, "The Mirage of an Unmarked Whiteness," 6.

[30] See Bryan Massingale, "The Case for Catholic Support: Catholic Social Ethics and Environmental Justice," in Hayes and Davis, *Taking Down Our Harps,* 157.

[31] Sylvia Hood Washington, *Packing Them In: An Archaeology of Environmental Racism in Chicago, 1865–1954* (New York: Lexington Books, 2005), 2.

[32] Ibid., 38.

[33] See Deborah Fins, "Death Row U.S.A.," in NAACP Legal Defense and Educational Fund, *Criminal Justice Project Quarterly Report* (Spring 2006): 3.

[34] Traci West, *Disruptive Christian Ethics: When Racism and Women's Lives Matter* (Louisville, KY: Westminster John Knox Press, 2006), 44.

[35] Peggy McIntosh, "Unpacking the Invisible Knapsack" (workshop, White Privilege: Implications for the Catholic University, the Church, and Theology Conference, University of Notre Dame, Notre Dame, IN, March 27, 2006).

[36] Diana L. Hayes, "And When We Speak: To Be Black, Catholic, and Womanist," in Hayes and Davis, *Taking Down Our Harps*, 113; see also Copeland, "The Exercise of Black Theology in the United States."

[37] Copeland, "Foundations for Catholic Theology in an African American Context," 132.

[38] Rosita deAnn Mathews, "Using Power from the Periphery: An Alternative Theological Model for Survival in Systems," in *A Troubling in My Soul: Womanist Perspectives on Evil and Suffering*, ed. Emilie M. Townes (Maryknoll, NY: Orbis Books, 1993), 99.

[39] Joanna Macy and Molly Young Brown, *Coming Back to Life: Practices to Reconnect Our Lives, Our World* (Gabriola Island, Canada: New Society Publishers, 1998), 53.

[40] Ibid.

[41] John Paul II, *Sollicitudo Rei Socialis*, 38. Emphasis in the original.

[42] *Populorum Progressio*, 23, in O'Brien and Shannon, *Catholic Social Thought*, 245. See also *Economic Justice for All*, 34: "*From the patristic period to the present, the Church has affirmed that misuse of the world's resources or appropriation of them by a minority of the world's population betrays the gift of creation since 'whatever belongs to God belongs to all'*" (emphasis in original) (O'Brien and Shannon, *Catholic Social Thought*, 586); *Sollicitudo Rei Socialis*, 42: "The *option* or *love of preference* for the poor . . . is an option, or a *special form* of primacy in the exercise of Christian charity, to which the whole tradition of the Church bears witness. It affects the life of each Christian inasmuch as he or she seeks to imitate the life of Christ, but it applies equally to our *social responsibilities* and hence to our manner of living, and to the logical decisions to be made concerning the ownership and use of goods. . . . It is necessary to state once more the characteristic principle of Christian social doctrine: the goods of this world are *originally meant for all*. The right to private property is *valid and necessary,* but it does not nullify the value of this principle. Private property, in fact, is under a 'social mortgage,' which means that it has an intrinsically social function, based upon and justified precisely by the principle of the universal destination of goods" (emphasis in the original) (O'Brien and Shannon, *Catholic Social Thought*, 425–26).

[43] See *The Divine Comedy,* "Inferno," Canto XVII, in *The Portable Dante*, ed. Mark Musa (New York: Penguin Books, 1995).

⁴⁴ Dorothee Soelle, *The Silent Cry: Mysticism and Resistance*, trans. Barbara and Martin Rumscheidt (Minneapolis: Fortress Press, 2001), 253.

⁴⁵ Cornel West, *Race Matters* (New York: Vintage Books, 1993), 10; see also 137.

⁴⁶ James W. Perkinson, *White Theology: Outing Supremacy in Modernity* (New York: Palgrave Macmillan, 2004), 234.

⁴⁷ Noel Ignatiev and John Garvey, eds., *Race Traitor* (New York: Routledge, 1996); see also Richard Delgado, "Rodrigo's Eleventh Chronicle: Empathy and False Empathy," in Delgado and Stefancic, *Critical White Studies*, 615.

⁴⁸ Frankenberg has noted the emergence among some white U.S. Americans of what she calls "power-evasive race cognizance" ("The Mirage of an Unmarked Whiteness," 90–91); see also Delgado, "Rodrigo's Eleventh Chronicle," 616–17.

⁴⁹ Jennifer Harvey, "Race and Reparations: The Material Logics of White Supremacy," in Harvey, Case, and Gorsline, *Disrupting White Supremacy from Within*, 113.

8

· · · ·

"BECOMING BLACK WITH GOD"

Toward an Understanding of the Vocation of the White Catholic Theologian in the United States

Laurie M. Cassidy

To define the vocation of the white Catholic theologian neces-sitates contending with the context of American culture and the global society that is rife with lethal racism. One of the primary theological tasks imposed by the crisis of this lethal racism is critical scholarly attention to understanding the reach and extent of white privilege.[1]

I agree with Shawn Copeland's diagnosis of racism as a spiri-tual wound that afflicts all who dwell in the house built on race.[2] She prescribes a deep rooting in the terrain of spirituality and practice in order for theologians to participate in the healing of this wound both personally and collectively.[3]

This diagnosis poses a dilemma for white theologians. One particular symptom of this wound of racism in white people is a perverse form of ignorance. Being white is having the privilege of functioning in society blind to the system into which one is born and from which one benefits. Part of what it means to be "white" involves the internalization of an epistemology that precludes self-transparency and genuine self-understanding of social relations in regard to race.[4] As Charles Mills explains, being white involves being born into a racial contract that is maintained by individual and collective "ignorance."

> Thus in effect, on matters related to race, the Racial Contract prescribes for its signatories an inverted epistemology, an epistemology of ignorance, a particular pattern of localized and global cognitive dysfunctions (which are psychologically and socially functional), producing the ironic outcome that whites will in general be unable to understand the world they themselves have made.[5]

This ignorance may manifest itself in white consciousness as a greater awareness of racial oppression shaping black experience rather than of the privilege shaping one's own life. White people may actually be attuned to discrimination against people of color while viewing their own life as racially neutral.[6] This view of being white as "colorless" has profound consequences for views of injustice. At best, a white person can view fighting racism as a compassionate work for "others," not something inexorably linked to his or her own "white" existence. At worst, a white person may reproduce and reinscribe the dominant power relations he or she believes should be changed. Without understanding and acknowledging white privilege, "racism can, in short, be conceived as something external . . . rather than as a system that shapes [the white person's] daily existence and sense of self."[7]

This perverse ignorance poses a theological problem for white theologians. In light of this epistemological blindness imposed by whiteness, how do white theologians take up the task of understanding the reach and extent of white privilege? I believe answering this question will entail spirituality, a spirituality that enables white theologians to see and understand the world that whiteness has made. Or, more specifically, a spirituality that will heal the wound in order to be able to take up the theological task of critically assessing and dismantling white privilege. In this article I explore the potential of James Cone's notion of "becoming Black with God" as a basis for developing such a spirituality. I argue that Cone's metaphor of "God is Black" holds a radically disclosive power to reveal. Cone's juxtaposition of "God" with "Black" is a theological lens allowing us to see whiteness in stark contrast with the God of Jesus. The attendant ethical demand to "become Black with God" signifies a way of being in the world, the way of God's grace and human salvation.

My intent here is not to offer a comprehensive account of the spirituality needed to dismantle white privilege. I believe the development of a spirituality that nurtures our capacity as white Catholic theologians to confront racism will be the result of collective praxis and critical reflection. My purpose here is to suggest a potent metaphor in the development of this spirituality. I begin with an explication and analysis of Cone's notion of "becoming Black with God." Cone intends his theology to be free of jargon. His straightforward language betrays a density that, upon analysis, serves up insight on the connections among developing authentic God language, living as image and likeness of God, and life in America. Following from my analysis I draw implications of Cone's work that deserve further study in developing a spirituality that may create the possibility to heal the wound caused by race.

James Cone:
"Becoming Black with God"

In 1970 James Cone declared that "God is Black."[8] God is black, Cone explains, "not just because African Americans are Black, but because God freely chooses to be known as the One who freely liberates victims from oppression."[9] The blackness of God signifies that the essence of God's nature is discovered in the activity of liberation.

> The Blackness of God means that God has made the oppressed condition God's own condition. This is the essence of the biblical liberation. By electing Israelite slaves as the people of God and by becoming the oppressed One in Jesus Christ, the human race is made to understand that God is known where human beings experience humiliation and suffering. It is not that God feels sorry and takes pity on them . . . quite the contrary, God's election of Israel and incarnation in Christ reveal that *liberation* of the oppressed is part of the innermost nature of God.[10]

Cone's declaration is replete with meaning about God's being and activity, not only as revealed in scripture but also as known in the history of the United States. God's blackness signifies not only the convergence of God's redemptive activity and black experience, but also the idolatry of using Christianity to justify white supremacy.

Cone's theological language attempts to make intelligible the religious experience of his enslaved ancestors. Though physically bound, African Americans experienced a God of freedom who broke through the distortions of the gospel used to spiritually bind and pacify slaves.[11] Rereading the Bible through these eyes, Cone develops a symbolic language to shock us into recognition not only of the plight of oppressed and oppressor, but also of God's liberating activity in the particularity of American history in behalf of African Americans.

Utilizing the theory of Paul Ricoeur, Diana Hayes argues that "God is Black" is a true metaphor. Hayes explains that the use of metaphor implies a twist or shift of meaning by creating language that turns the world upside down. This subversive language brings together ideas thought to be incompatible.[12] According to Hayes, Cone's metaphor works because it juxtaposes two realities thought to be unrelated in America—divinity and black experience. This juxtaposition of God with black enables a new vision of reality—ultimate reality and historical reality.

> No one is shocked to hear that God/Christ may be White, that has been the prevailing assumption of the Western world. . . . It is in just that juxtaposition of one reality with another which is totally, in the position of many, not only unrelated but actually almost heretical that the metaphor is born and that it works: "the metaphorical meaning instituted a 'proximity' between significations which were hitherto distant. . . . It is from this proximity that a new vision of reality springs up, one which is resisted by ordinary language tied to the ordinary use of words."[13]

Cone's metaphor challenges us with a new vision of reality, one that may be difficult for white theologians to see. In claiming God's blackness, Cone raises the question of the reach and extent of white privilege and the theological vocation. His metaphor uncovers the relationship among the symbols that inform faith experience, the capacity to create authentic God language, and racism. More pointedly, I see in Cone's metaphor the question of how the social locations of whiteness have shaped white people's spiritual lives. Cone is not only interpreting God's liberating presence in black experience, but also by declaring that God is black he calls into question the assumed whiteness of God. Unveiling this idolatrous assumption questions the normativity of white people's existence by striking at the source of its religious legitimization. To probe the depth of Cone's challenge is to come to grips with the complex problem of the "invisibility" of whiteness.

To use the term *white* is not only to speak of literal skin pigment, but also to refer to a complex set of social locations that are historically, socially, politically, and culturally produced. Moreover, *white* and *whiteness* refer to how these locations are linked to unfolding relations of power and domination.[14] Though this power is uneven in that it is conditioned by factors such as gender and class, "among the effects on white people both of race privilege and of the dominance of whiteness are their seeming normativity, and their structured invisibility."[15] This seeming normativity engenders an ignorance in white people of the privileges entailed in white existence. Simple examples of this unacknowledged privilege abound in daily life. For instance, white people call 911 and can expect that help will come quickly.[16]

To grow up as a white person in America is a complex process that involves internalizing the assumption of the normativity of one's racial existence. This normativity of whiteness functions by being invisible to white people. To use the term *whiteness* is to displace the location of being white as unmarked and invisible and to bring it to a place of visibility. Through naming whiteness, the raced social location of being white comes into view, calling its normativity into question.

I believe Cone's language is profoundly helpful in making the theological and moral implications of whiteness visible to white theologians. To say that God is black poses the question of white privilege as a theological problem, not only a social, political, and cultural location of power and domination. Cone's God-language brings into stark contrast the idolatrous supposition of white as an assumed divine referent. To say "God is Black" is to reveal that assuming "God is white" is how faith functions to legitimate the complex dominant systems that privilege people with white skin. The depth of this legitimization is profound yet so subtle that to be white and Christian in America usually means never having to question the color of God's face. Examining the seditious inner reach of white privilege in terms of personal faith brings home the reality that the wound of racism is not a problem "out there" but rather one that imprints itself on the human spirit.

Moreover, Cone's God-language also discloses the connection between one's image of God and moral imagination. The dynamics of moral imagination can be described as a lens and a filter.[17] Imagination orients one to choose and notice details, make sense of those details, and form patterns from disparate elements. "People imagine their world into being. We compose the world we find."[18] So, too, for theologians; we compose the world we find. Cone's metaphor brings into focus the truth that black human beings are made in the image and likeness of God. Cone's metaphor acts as a lens that informs white theologians' moral imagination and attempts to correct what has been filtered out. It is humbling to recognize that white privilege has made white theologians unable to notice the theological significance of the suffering of black human beings, which is "arguably the most persistent and insidious human rights issue in America."[19] It is troubling, too, that white privilege blinds white theologians to the patterns that connect white existence and black suffering.

Cone writes that the only way we can authentically explore these theological and moral issues is by "becoming Black with God." Cone explains, "Knowing God means being on the side of the oppressed, becoming *one* with them, and participating in the goal of liberation. *We must become black with God!*" (emphasis in original).[20] To know God's inner nature and activity in the world necessitates participating in the activity of liberation. Knowing who God is comes from discipleship, from activity in solidarity with the oppressed. For Cone, to become black with God is not simply psychological identification with the "other" or empathy for the suffering of the oppressed. To become black with God "is identification of one's destiny with that of others and a choice of sides."[21] According to Cone, God has made the oppressed's destiny God's own destiny; therefore, to know God we must make the destiny of the oppressed our destiny.

Cone explores the existential and theological conundrum of a white person becoming black. He explains that blackness and salvation are synonymous. Salvation—to become black—is the work of God, not a human work. To become black is a question of faith and belief, which is not a human accomplishment but a divine gift.

> To *believe* is to receive the gift and utterly to reorient one's existence on the basis of the gift. The gift is so unlike what humans expect that when it is offered and accepted, we become completely new creatures. This is what the wholly Otherness of God means. God comes to us in God's blackness, which is wholly unlike whiteness. To receive God's revelation is to become black with God by joining God in the work of liberation.[22]

According to Cone, "to become Black with God" is not a physical change but an ontological change that makes the believer capable of participating in God's work of liberating the oppressed. To work with God for liberation is not an addition to what saves us but is itself human salvation. What makes this saving transformation possible is God's grace.

I do not subscribe to the essentialist view of race that is implied in Cone's theology.[23] However, I argue that his ontology is theological language that attempts to account for the profound transformation that is necessary for white people to embark on the task of not only acknowledging but also relinquishing white privilege and living in solidarity with the oppressed. The mandate "to become Black with God" implies that white theologians will comprehend the reach of white privilege by being drawn by God into God's activity of liberating the oppressed in the world.

I acknowledge the limits of Cone's construction, even though his God-language has expanded.[24] Cone's claim to ontological blackness renders black life monolithic.[25] To be black, as well as to be white, deserves complex forms of analysis that account for the tension of holding simultaneous roles of oppressed and oppressor.[26] Cone's logic also sets blackness and whiteness in binary opposition, which engenders many problems, not the least of which is that such duality ignores the complex reality of people of color in the United States.[27] I do not believe these critiques compromise Cone's challenge for us to explore critically how white privilege subverts the theological task of creating God language. To say "God is Black" and "we must become black with God" not only discloses whiteness as a theological problem for white theologians but also suggests a profound spiritual journey.

Implication for a Spirituality That Dismantles White Privilege

In this final section I explore implications that Cone's construction offers for a spirituality to dismantle white privilege.

First, I believe Cone's work challenges theologians to examine the consequences of how white theologians imagine God in prayer. Cone's construction suggests the connection between the God we pray to and our moral imagination. In "The Mystery of Being Human Together," Mary Aquin O'Neil explores the theological connection between divine imagery and human identification. She explores this connection through the lens of gender oppression. O'Neil explains that exclusively male imagery of the divine not only compromises women's capacity to find their image and likeness in God as creator and redeemer but also handicaps men from viewing women as *imago Dei*. Through her gender analysis O'Neil demonstrates the connections among God-language, theological anthropology, and moral imagination. O'Neil's research brings her to ask a challenging question: "Is it too strong to say that one who cannot find the other in God cannot love the other as she or he is? I think not."[28] Borrowing O'Neil's line of reasoning, is it too strong to say that if we cannot imagine God being black we cannot truly love black human beings as they are? I think not.

O'Neil's profound question leads us to explore the integral relationship between prayer and moral imagination in the dynamic of white privilege. Taking seriously Cone's insight may suggest praying to God—who is black. If God's inner nature is known in God's becoming one with the oppressed, God's countenance will resemble the likeness of those most oppressed in our society. For example, to encounter God in prayer may suggest

God's female face as ebony and wrinkled with age as she embraces her grandchildren orphaned by AIDS. What would it be like to contemplate the face of God as poor, black, and female? This prayer suggests not only our gazing at God, but also this black grandmother-God gazing at us. I believe God's gazing upon us, with the pain of the world in her eyes, holds the power of healing the blindness of white privilege. The imprint of this gaze upon us has the power to make white theologians black with God.

Utilizing Cone's metaphor reveals the radically social character of personal prayer. His metaphor is subversive because it affects how we understand the nature of God; our understanding of God is what imprints the character and quality of our human life.[29]

Second, I believe Cone's dialectical imagination resonates with the dialectical elements of Christian spirituality, particularly Carmelite spirituality. Cone's dialectical imagination and his ontological language suggest God as wholly Other and salvation as a graced process of radical transformation, which I see as resonant with the "dark night" of John of the Cross.

The darkness of John's night is the in-flow of God. As Carmelite scholar Constance FitzGerald explains, "Dark night is not primarily *some thing*, an impersonal darkness like a difficult situation or distressful psychological condition, but *someone*, a presence leaving an indelible imprint on the human spirit and consequently one's entire life."[30] Here, darkness is the divine Other who is drawing humans into intimacy. In this God-imagery darkness is retrieved from its negative use in Christianity.[31] John's dark God is wholly Other, incomprehensible, all good, and all loving. John's description, like Cone's metaphor, subverts the connection of dark and black as insinuating dirt, filth, guilt, or moral degradation, which have become connected to black humanity. Moreover, John is describing God and God's desire to subvert one's beliefs, one's sense of self, and one's relation to the world— a world conditioned by systems of dominance and subordination. John describes a God deeply at work to radically transform the human heart. The imprint of divine love upon the human heart subverts our sustaining involvement in relations of dominance and subordination.

The wisdom of the dialectical perspective in both James Cone and John of the Cross is that it takes seriously the impotence of human will in overcoming encrusted social sin and evil. This wisdom exposes the desperate need for grace in the struggle to overcome the virulent blindness of white privilege. In his writings John of the Cross describes how God's passionate drawing of the human heart transforms desire and affectivity. For John, it is the imprint of this "dark" God in human consciousness that subverts deeply rooted attachments and frees human beings for love.

FitzGerald interprets the transformational process of the dark night as producing a "participatory epistemology," a love-knowledge of the world that enables us to see the world through God's eyes because our capacity to relate to the world has radically changed.[32] Addressing the blindness of white privilege through the writings of James Cone and John of the Cross suggests that overcoming this epistemological blindness will not involve simply revealing what is now unseen, but rather radical change in the capacity to relate to self, to God, and to others. Seeing and acknowledging white privilege come from the grace of relationships that imprint a new way of being upon human consciousness.

Conclusion

Cone's metaphor is revelatory not because it provides answers to white theologians about white privilege. Rather, Cone's metaphor is revealing because it offers central questions that challenge white theologians to interrogate the connections of whiteness and the experience of God. I believe struggling to answer these questions draws white theologians into a journey with God that will make possible a life in solidarity with the oppressed. In such a journey we will realize solidarity as constitutive of our theological vocation, and, if Cone is right, be saved.

Notes

[1] M. Shawn Copeland, "Racism and the Vocation of the Christian Theologian," *Spiritus* 2, no. 1 (2002): 25.

[2] Ibid., 21.

[3] Ibid., 25.

[4] Charles Mills, *The Racial Contract* (Ithaca, NY: Cornell University Press, 1997), 18.

[5] Ibid., 18.

[6] Ruth Frankenberg, *White Women, Race Matters: The Social Construction of Whiteness* (Minneapolis: University of Minnesota Press, 1993), 49.

[7] Ibid., 6.

[8] James H. Cone, *A Black Theology of Liberation* (1970; reprint Maryknoll, NY: Orbis Books, 1986, 1990).

[9] James H. Cone, "God Is Black," in *Constructing Christian Theologies from the Underside* ed. Susan Brooks Thistlewaite and Mary Potter Engel (San Francisco: Harper Collins, 1990), 82.

[10] Cone, *A Black Theology of Liberation*, 64.

[11] James H. Cone, "An African American Perspective on the Cross and Suffering," in *The Scandal of the Crucified World: Perspectives on the Cross and Suffering*, ed. Yacob Tesfai (Maryknoll, NY: Orbis Books, 1986), 64.

[12] Diana L. Hayes, "James Cone's Hermeneutic of Language and Black Theology," *Theological Studies* 61 (2000): 619.

[13] Paul Ricoeur, "Biblical Hermeneutics," *Semeia* 13 (1975): 80, quoted in ibid.

[14] Frankenberg, *White Women, Race Matters*, 6.

[15] Ibid.

[16] "911 is a joke/Everyday they don't never come correct/you can ask my man right here with a broken neck/He's a witness to the job never bein' done/" (Public Enemy, "911 Is a Joke," *Fear of a Black Planet* [New York: Def Jam Recordings, 1990]).

[17] Sharon Parks, *The Critical Years* (New York: Harper and Row, 1986), 116.

[18] Ibid. For more on the connection of moral imagination and the theological task of redressing racism, see Margaret Eletta Guider, "Moral Imagination and *Missio ad Gentes*: Redressing the Counterwitness of Racism," *Proceedings of the Catholic Theological Society of America* 56 (2001): 49–69.

[19] Bryan Massingale, "The African American Experience and U.S. Roman Catholic Ethics: 'Strangers and Aliens No Longer?'" in *Black and Catholic: The Challenge and Gift of Black Folk*, ed. Jamie T. Phelps (Milwaukee: Marquette University Press, 1997), 86.

[20] Cone, *A Black Theology of Liberation*, 65.

[21] Ibid., 63.

[22] Cone, "God Is Black," 87.

[23] I contend that race is an unstable complex of social meanings that are undergoing constant change as a result of political struggle.

For more on this view of race, see Michael Omi and Howard Winant, *Racial Formation in the United States from the 1960s to the 1990s* (New York: Routledge, 1994), 55. What I am advocating is white theologians' commitment to the sustained analysis necessary to study these changing complex processes.

[24] In 1990 Cone described the inclusive quality of his metaphor "God is Black": "I still believe that 'God is Black' in the sense that God's identity is found in the faces of those who are exploited and humiliated because of their color. But I also believe that 'God is mother,' 'rice,' 'red,' and a host of other things that give life to those whom society condemns to death. 'Black,' 'mother,' 'rice' and 'red' give concreteness to God's life-giving presence in the world and re-mind us that the universality of God is found in the particularity of the suffering poor" (Cone, "God Is Black," 83).

[25] Victor Anderson, *Beyond Ontological Blackness: An Essay on African American Religious and Cultural Criticism* (New York: Continuum, 1995), 11, 12.

[26] Womanists critique the sexism of Cone's original construction; for example, see Kelly Brown Douglas, *The Black Christ* (Maryknoll, NY: Orbis Books, 1994), 91–92.

[27] Anderson, *Beyond Ontological Blackness*, 91–93. The construction of my argument may appear to replicate the binary thinking I say I reject. A conviction that I bring to this article is that this binary opposition of black and white as regards race will not be overcome until America confronts the history and impact of the enslavement of African people. It may be that in dealing with African enslavement and the genocide of indigenous peoples as America's "original sin," we white Americans will be given the grace that opens our eyes to see and engage all the kinds of difference in us and around us. For an ethical framework in which differences can be understood and valued, see Wendy Farley, *Eros for the Other: Retaining Truth in a Pluralistic World* (University Park: Pennsylvania State University Press, 1996).

[28] Mary Aquin O'Neil, "The Mystery of Being Human Together," in *Freeing Theology: The Essentials of Theology in Feminist Perspective*, ed. Catherine Mowry LaCugna (New York: Harper Collins, 1993), 159.

[29] This insight on the connection between understanding God and the character of human life is from Constance FitzGerald, "Transformation in Wisdom: The Subversive Character and Educative Power

of Sophia in Contemplation," in *Carmel and Contemplation: Transforming Human Consciousness*, ed. Kevin Culligan and Regis Jordan (Washington, DC: ICS Publications, 2000), 284.

[30] Ibid., 310.

[31] For a study of the role of blackness and darkness within Christianity, see Robert Hood, *"Begrimed and Black": Christian Traditions on Blacks and Blackness* (Minneapolis: Fortress Press, 1990).

[32] FitzGerald, "Transforming Wisdom," 310–13.

9

• • • •

(UN)LEARNING WHITE MALE IGNORANCE

Alex Mikulich

White male theologians stand at a historical and theological crossroads, to draw upon M. Shawn Copeland's imaginative trope, where we should no longer evade the permanent achievements of black Catholic theology and the dangerous memory of Jesus. We stand at a crossroads where we can no longer evade the U.S. legacy of slavery, racism, and persistent white racial privilege that obscures the rich history and memory of the "uncommon faithfulness" of African American Catholics.[1]

Copeland recalls the legacy of blues master Robert Johnson, who calls blues musicians to bring their instruments to the "crossroads" at midnight for re-tuning by "the Bluesman." Similarly, she invites each of us to bring our hearts to the crossroads where "heaven and earth meet" before the cross of Jesus, where our hearts may experience graced re-tuning, individually and collectively. At the present historical crossroads of societal impasse as a "dark night" of the soul, in multiple forms of social and moral decline, Copeland passionately invites us to re-tune our lives to one another and God.[2] If we walk to the crossroads where the dangerous memory of the community of faith forms at the cross of Jesus, we may yet gain the grace to re-tune our hearts and accept the gift and challenge of reconciliation.

I approach this crossroads as a white male U.S. citizen who systematically benefits from structured racial, gender, and class privilege. I benefit psychologically, materially, and socially from hierarchies of gender and race that result in lethal racism. I also wonder what lies beyond the limits and privilege of my location. What possibility is there that we white male theologians will acknowledge our complicity in the social sin of white privilege and seek communal repentance? When and how will we collectively acknowledge, celebrate, and learn from the wisdom, insight, and experience of our black, Latina, and First American brothers and sisters?

Drawing upon M. Shawn Copeland's praxis of solidarity, I reinterpret Nicholas of Cusa's spirituality of *learned ignorance* as a way of being with "society's most abject" before the cross of Jesus. I begin by introducing Nicholas of Cusa's notion of *learned ignorance* as a spiritual path that comprises three forms of ignorance. The main body of my essay reinterprets Cusa's learned ignorance through Copeland's praxis of solidarity as a way to address white male privilege. A praxis of solidarity also demands a pedagogy that immerses white male theologians in the terror faced by peoples of color. Drawing upon the work of James W. Perkinson, I contend that unlearning white male ignorance involves a pedagogy of seeing ourselves in the mirror of blackness.

A pedagogy of unlearning white privilege and a praxis of solidarity before the cross may offer the possibility that white male theologians will take responsibility for our complicity in oppression and seek communal repentance for our sinfulness. At this crossroads white male theologians may yet pursue the grace of Cusa's "wise fools" and learned ignorance of the many ways that black Catholics, African Americans, Latinas, and First Peoples of the Americas have transformed Christianity and democracy itself.[3]

Nicholas of Cusa on Learned Ignorance

The fundamental idea of learned ignorance is not a general ignorance that devalues learning; rather, Nicholas invites us to strive along a path of "instructed wisdom" as the "wisdom of not knowing" that results in wonder before the "divine Unity in diversity."[4] Cusa's "wisdom of not knowing" is instructed by human comparison to the perfection of divine wisdom "in which everything is united."[5] Hugh Lawrence Bond explains that, for

Cusa, ignorance does not provide an end, "but way and mediation, access and entry." Cusa writes, "[Learned ignorance] is the
way of wonder, and like contemplation it is receptivity to mystery, and the end remains forever unspeakable and incomprehensible: beyond knowing and not knowing, God and not God, never
merely God."[6] As a way of receptivity to mystery, instructed wisdom invites a constant wonder and humility throughout life that
recognizes "that to which one turns one's love" is the infinite
source of all knowing, being, and loving.[7]

Nicholas posits three different forms of ignorance. First, he
describes the ignorance of those who trust in their human intelligence and who through pride and presumptuousness close themselves off from the path of divine wisdom. This is the worst form
of ignorance because it represents a smug knowing that stands
irresponsive to the divine origin of the "tree of life." Theologically, unlearned ignorance involves a fundamental absence to
oneself, others, God, and the whole of God's creation. Nicholas
names people "unwise fools" who in "their vanities fell short
and embraced the tree of knowledge but did not apprehend the
tree of life."[8]

Nicholas describes a second form of ignorance as the basic
reality of human finitude and incapacity to know or name God
as God is—the human acknowledgment of God's utter transcendence. As Cusa compares the finitude of human knowing to God's
knowing and loving, he recognizes that knowledge is "utterly
restricted to knowing only those things that bear some comparison or proportion to what is present in one's own realm."[9] The
relationship between human finitude and divine transcendence
reveals a tension between the limits of human reason and a knowing or vision that lies beyond all discursive knowledge.

Ignorance becomes learned when the tension between discursive knowledge and that which lies beyond is maintained.[10] The
tension of learned ignorance reveals a relationship between human beings and God. Learned ignorance means recognizing oneself as ignorant in relationship to the infinity of divine truth. The
"knowing" of this ignorance in relationship reveals something
more: human beings are known more by God than we are able to
know. God's infinite knowing reveals who we are to ourselves,
God, and all others.

Most important, learned ignorance implies a conversion into a way of living in humble worship and desire to live for Truth itself. The conversion of learned ignorance becomes evident in two modes of Cusanus's prayer. First, a tone of humility in his prayer stresses the tendency of the soul, when thrown back to the limits of human knowing, "to abnegate itself in that state of wonder called forth by the idea of God." Second, Nicholas's recognition of this condition of humility and wonder leads to the realization that the intercession of grace "gives the soul the ability to approach the vision of God more closely."[11] The grace of contemplative prayer becomes "united to the action of returning to God."[12] Cusa unites contemplation and action because "God reveals himself as if he were our creature, so that when we see him, we see ourselves whom we love. And it is this love which God uses to draw us back to [God]." The prayer of learned ignorance, initiated by God's love, marks a shift beyond all forms of knowing and becomes a way of being or a stance in the world that humbly reveres the source of being, living, and understanding itself.[13]

"Illumined ignorance," Cusa's third form of ignorance, retains the reality of human finitude and unknowing but *gains illumination through the sight of another*. For Nicholas, illumination comes only through God's seeing Godself in and through us. Cusa's notion of sight involves much more than physical seeing; ultimately, God's vision reveals the depth and breadth of our identity in relationship to God and others. Cusa states that the "being of a creature is equally [God's] seeing and [God] being seen."[14]

Louis Dupré explains that "for Cusanus mystical *seeing* does not imply the objectifying effect which we commonly associate with visual activity." Rather, "God's *seeing*" reveals "to creatures their innermost reality wherein they themselves become *seeing*."[15] "God's seeing" as the "innermost reality" of being human simultaneously includes our dependence upon God creating us, sustaining us, and God's presence to us with and through all others.[16] For Nicholas, God's illumination of learned ignorance draws us into the full realization of ourselves as rooted in God's being and love.

The reconciliation of human ignorance with God's seeing becomes possible only through God's self-disclosure in Jesus Christ.

The incarnation reveals the full possibility of being human, of knowing ourselves and others through God's loving presence. Jesus draws us through faith to ourselves and to a practical way of living that reveals God's love in and through all others. The life of faith in "illumined ignorance" means that "what is done to one of the least is done to Christ" in and through whom "each member will be one with God."[17] Ultimately, for Nicholas, Jesus Christ is the condition of the possibility of knowing God and the epistemological ground for every theological effort, every act of faith, and every act of love.[18]

Nicholas's life witnesses to the illumination of ignorance realized in prayer and love of others. Before his death Nicholas executed a foundation deed for a hospital at Kues that he intended to serve as a refuge and *hospitale pauperum* for thirty-three poor men.[19] That hospital still stands as Nicholas's legacy. For Cusa, God's compassionate gaze in and through all others intensifies our desire for God in prayer and our desire to witness to God's love in action. The contemplative practice of God's compassionate gaze reveals who we are in relationship with ourselves, all others, and God. Moreover, the illumined ignorance of all these relationships reveals how the entire universe is rooted in the divine "tree of life."

M. Shawn Copeland's Praxis of Solidarity before the Cross

Cusanus scholars, beware: I do not intend to follow Nicholas on a neoplatonic ascent to God. Instead, I reinterpret learned ignorance through M. Shawn Copeland's theology of the cross that invites social, political, and economic solidarity with "despised poor women of color" to offer a more practical, embodied way to walk the way of the cross and journey into learned ignorance.[20] Reinterpreted through Copeland's praxis of solidarity before the cross of Jesus, I draw fundamentally upon Nicholas's notion of learned ignorance as a spirituality or a way for white male theologians to interrupt our privilege, root ourselves in an authentic humanity, and learn how our African, Latina, Native American, and black Catholic brothers and sisters witness to a way of living and traditions that embrace the "tree of life." A white male pedagogy of learned ignorance entails reversing the modern gaze of white supremacy, a reversal that whites may pursue only by looking into the mirror of blackness. Walking the way of learned ignorance means seeing ourselves as our black, Latina, and First American brothers and sisters see us.

Like Cusa's approach to learned ignorance, Copeland approaches solidarity as a way of prayer and as a fundamental way of being in love with God in the world. She insists with Gustavo Gutiérrez that theology is always a second step to the life of faith. As theologians, we must plant ourselves "in the terrain of spirituality and practice."[21] The theologian's ultimate commitment can never be to any institution or structure, person or group, "but only to the God of Jesus Christ."[22] The prophetic praxis of Jesus "demonstrates the risk and meaning of a life lived in prayerful hope."[23] Prayer that directs us to the prophetic praxis of Jesus passionately reaches for risks and launches us into a lifelong journey where we may discover and yet be transformed into the Divine Unknown—"the only future worth hoping for and having."[24]

This spirituality reorients us to a transformative way of being in the world. It nurtures us in prayerful "silence, stillness, attention, [and] reverence" before God as it interrupts all forms of pettiness, selfishness, smug knowledge, and illegitimate power. Our present crossroad of social decline demands nurturing ourselves in silent, still, attentive, and reverent love of God. Copeland calls us in this wellspring of loving prayer to respond to Jesus' invitation to "come and see,"[25] to listen to others in their particularity, to learn from others in their wisdom, to live authentically in the graced presence of all others where we may yet glimpse the fullness of life God intends for all.

This passionate way of prayer and being in the world reveals the love of Jesus, of self, others, and the whole of God's creation in the praxis of solidarity. Solidarity begins practically through the "intentional remembering of the dead exploited, despised poor peoples of color." Intentional remembering "cannot be pietistic or romantic" for such "engagement of the histories of suffering is fraught with ambiguity and paradox." The victims of history are lost yet we live because "*we owe* all that we have" to the "exploitation and enslavement, removal and extermination of women and men of color."[26] Our debt "uncovers our anxiety" because our "'own existence becomes a self-contradiction by means of the solidarity to which it is indebted.'"[27]

Africans in diaspora and African American Christianity practiced "dangerous memories" of their African and Christian narratives and ancestors long before this category was ever created in modern critical theory or political theology. As Shawn Copeland and many others have so carefully recorded, Africans in diaspora, First Americans, and Mestizos practiced, and continue to practice, living dangerous memory of their narratives and ancestors as a way of life through which they "claimed their subjectivity [and] exercised their agency."[28]

Copeland's praxis of solidarity invites learned ignorance by learning from and struggling with women of color who suffer racial, economic, and gender exploitation. This praxis of solidarity and memory of the cross of Jesus create a dynamic rooted in religious, intellectual, and moral conversion that may transform us yet into our shared, authentic humanity and personhood. Solidarity reveals the universality of God's love by recognizing and regarding "exploited, poor women of color for who they are— God's own creation."[29] Drawing upon Lonergan, she stresses that liberation theologies push us to realize that

> humanity is one intelligible reality—multiple, diverse, varied, and concrete, yet one. Whether white or red or yellow or brown or black, whether male or female, whether Irish or British, Australian or Japanese, Canadian or Somalian, human beings are intrinsically, metaphysically, ineluctably connected.[30]

Notice that for Copeland and the liberation theologies she draws upon, the turn to poor women of color is not grounded in political calculation, correctness, or reaction, nor does it exhibit any trace of *ressentiment* or intent to alienate those who are white, powerful, privileged, and/or male.[31] She recognizes that if this turn to poor women of color was intended for political ends or to alienate any person or group, "it would be little more than ideology as crude justification or a repeat of the desecration of the *humanum*."[32] Rather, the risk of this turn "places us on the path of grace" that cannot be reduced to "even the most just arrangement of society."[33]

(Un)Learning White Male Ignorance
on the Way of Solidarity

Our Christian theological vocation calls us to take responsibility for white male privilege by walking the way of learned ignorance, a path that can only be found and endured if we walk humbly the way of the cross. The orientation, possibility, and transformative power of this journey are nothing other than God's love for us through Jesus Christ. We are called as theologians and members of the body of Christ to walk the way of the tensions, contradictions, doubts, fears, and risks of "working through whiteness,"[34] of acknowledging and subverting our participation in structures of privilege and exclusion, to open us up to the radical, transformative love of the cross. Only by walking the way of the cross may we gain insight into our ignorance of the ways white male privilege erodes our common humanity and nurture; as Margaret Guider observed, "to participate requires a willingness to approach, rather than avoid and evade, the discomfort, frustration, awkwardness, unmasking, exposure, misunderstanding, and vulnerability that forthright dialogue about the realities of racism and strategies for advancing racial justice inevitably elicits."[35]

Walking a way of solidarity and learned ignorance means living the tension between receiving the gift of God's infinite love and the task of resisting, disrupting, and dismantling the culture of lethal racism that white male theologians and ethicists perpetuate and from which we benefit.[36] Walking this journey means "working through" the contradictions between our claims for a universal ontological human equality and the reality of the social, political, and economic privilege that white theologians and ethicists consciously and unconsciously accept and assume.

The grace of this way may lure us yet into the "illumined ignorance" of communal lament and authentic communion "founded in the radical truth of our personal and collective history of joy and sorrow."[37] Becoming a repentant community will be no easy task, for it challenges white theologians to acknowledge our complicity in the ongoing legacy of Christian conquest of the peoples of the Americas and the multiple ways our continued acceptance of white privilege undermines the struggle of Native American,

African, Latina, and *mestizo* women and men in their struggle for self-determination.[38] The grace of this way lures us to re-pattern our way of being in the world and how we contribute to a Christian church that becomes a repentant community.

Contemporary acceptance of white male privilege, consciously or unconsciously, represents Nicholas's first form of ignorance. Unlearned ignorance, in Nicholas's terms, represents a foolishness that smacks of smug knowledge that remains unresponsive to the divine tree of life. It is curious that whites have failed to respond to Dr. Martin Luther King Jr.'s call "to re-educate themselves out of their racial ignorance. It is an aspect of their sense of superiority that the white people of America believe they have so little to learn."[39] I am continually learning how my life, the life of the American Catholic church, and the academy remain marked by scotosis, by blindness both to white male privilege and to the rich cultural, intellectual, religious, moral, and political contributions of black Catholics throughout American history. To quote Shawn Copeland:

> When will White Catholic theologians acknowledge the insights of Black theology as a permanently valid theological achievement? What other name can one give to this refusal and exclusion of Black insights but scotosis? White racist supremacy is the scotoma of Catholic theology. If there is a need for serious and exacting Black Catholic theology that goes well beyond historical retrieval, there is an even more urgent need for White Catholic theologians to critique White racist supremacy within Church and society.[40]

Bernard Lonergan's notion of bias or scotosis appropriately describes the unlearned ignorance of white male privilege. Lonergan describes scotosis as "an aberration of understanding" that results in a blind spot or scotoma, in which persons or groups refuse to submit their "own insights to the criticism based on others' experience and development."[41] Unlearned ignorance involves more than various forms of ignoring or denying white racial privilege—it fundamentally entails denying how our human identity is rooted in the divine tree of life that nurtures us through our African, Latino, and Native American brothers and sisters.

Theologically, put in Cusa's terms, the stakes of unlearned ignorance of white male privilege concern a fundamental absence to myself, others, and God. In Copeland's terms, unlearned ignorance entails inauthenticity before myself, others, and Jesus. Unlearned ignorance of white male privilege bespeaks an absence, if not a refusal, to participate in God's being and love. In Copeland's appropriation of Lonergan, unlearned ignorance of white male privilege involves a refusal to "Be attentive! Be intelligent! Be loving! Be responsible!" Unlearned ignorance of gender and racial privilege blocks the possibilities of individual and communal transcendence and conversion.

The stakes of unlearned ignorance further entail denial of our historical self-identity and interdependence with other human beings. White privilege accepts ignorance of our cultural, national, and theological dependence upon and rootedness in Africans, Latinos/as, and First Peoples of the Americas. It involves an ignorance, unconsciousness, or refusal to understand our interconnectedness with other human beings and how economically advantaged whites systematically benefit in the United States from structured racial hierarchies that are visible in health care, housing, educational attainment, criminal justice, and environmental quality.[42]

Jon Nilson situates the Catholic evasion of black theology in the convergence of defining moments for both the Roman Catholic Church and the black struggle for justice in the United States. Yet, in all of the reasons that Jon Nilson elaborates to explain the context of the Catholic evasion of black theology over the past forty years, he concludes that these reasons

are not "good" in the sense of exculpatory. They are not good enough to refute the charge of racism, however benevolent our racism has been. They are not good enough because they have led to our failure in solidarity, as Shawn Copeland describes it: "the empathetic incarnation of Christian love [that] . . . entails the recognition of our humanity of the 'other' as humanity, along with regard for the 'other" in her (and his) own otherness." And they are not good enough because this systemic White Catholic theological racism threatens our credentials. Our failure in solidarity means that we have failed in significant ways to live up to our vocation as Catholic theologians.[43]

Practicing solidarity before the cross of Jesus invites a way of humility and the possibility for white male theologians to become "learned fools." Solidarity invites humility before all others who have given us life and who reveal God's infinite love through history. If we hope to gain the grace of Cusa's instructed wisdom, we should heed Barbara Hilkert Andolsen's invitation (published before Peggy McIntosh's "White Privilege: Unpacking the Invisible Knapsack") to listen humbly to the experience, wisdom, and insight of our black, Latina, and Native American brothers and sisters.[44]

If white male theologians are going to become aware of our ignorance of how whiteness operates, *we need to see ourselves as others see us*. Whites generally live today in a kind of "'artless ignornance,' an almost incorrigible lack of awareness of either one's racial position or the actual cost to others of one's prosperity."[45] The art of educating ourselves into a learned ignorance of our racial position, as a spiritual and moral art, involves learning to see how our embodied seeing is far less than innocent, humanly, racially, theologically, and morally.[46]

A spiritual and moral art of white learned ignorance, especially for theologians, demands reversing the modern gaze of white supremacy. How could an insouciant whiteness reverse the modern gaze of supremacy? The question is ludicrous unless whites view ourselves from the perspective of black "double-consciousness." W. E. B. Du Bois describes the experience of black double-consciousness as always feeling "his two-ness, an American, a Negro; two souls, two thoughts, two un-reconciled strivings; two warring ideals in one dark body, whose dogged strength alone keeps it from being torn asunder."[47] This "doubling," this war, reverts back to its source: whiteness. James W. Perkinson argues that whites must look into the mirror of black double-consciousness and see the "ugly human" experienced by Du Bois.[48] Whites need to understand Malcolm X's insight that whiteness is demonic as a system or, as Du Bois put it, *"whiteness is the ownership of the earth forever and ever, Amen!"*[49] Looking into the mirror of double-consciousness demands an "encounter [by whites] with *whiteness as terror* in the mirror of blackface" that "sets the necessary tone for all the necessary work that must be done in exorcising supremacy, confessing history, and remaking community."[50] Unlearning white male ignorance means facing whiteness as the "demon in the eye of theology, what looks out from that eye, as it devours the world in its rapacious organizing gaze."[51] Ultimately, an artful path of white learned ignorance into black double-consciousness is soteriological, because "white anxiety will find its release only in facing the terror from which 'whiteness' itself has arisen in the first place."[52] In Shawn Copeland's words, white privilege is the "beam in the eye of our global village" that "poses a most dangerous threat to [the] realization of the body of Christ, to the reign of God."[53]

We need to see ourselves as our black, African, Latina, and Native American brothers and sisters have seen us through five hundred years of conquest, domination, and distortion of their humanity and ours.[54] Memory of the suffering of Jesus and our African and African American ancestors offers a practical way that white male theologians may root ourselves in the tree of life and the illumination of our shared, authentic communion in Jesus Christ. White male theologians may easily perpetuate our dominative role if we view memory simply as another intellectual category in the archives of twentieth-century European theology. If we contend with Antonio Gramsci's warning that we have been shaped by an "infinity of historical traces"[55] of which we remain unaware, retrieving the history and memory of Africans in diaspora, Mestizos, and First Peoples of the Americas offers critical insight into our common heritage.

Living memory reveals how our existence as white male theologians "becomes a self-contradiction by means of the solidarity to which it is indebted."[56] Whether we acknowledge it or not, white male privilege entails a fundamental contradiction in our existence because our privilege betrays the peoples who have formed the tree of life of our history, culture, and economy.

The problem for white male theologians becomes whether or not we work through this contradiction. We cannot endure, much less change, these contradictions by ourselves, but we can work through the contradictions of whiteness by crossing geographical, racial, gender, and class boundaries that separate us from one another and the love of God. Should we risk working through these contradictions at these crossroads, our brothers and sisters

can offer critiques of our present praxis of Christianity and democracy as they invite us to retrieve the fullness of our particular
and common humanity.

I conclude by returning to the crossroads of our theological
vocation. We are called, in Shawn Copeland's words, to recognize
Jesus' presence in the "suffering of Indians, blacks, and *mestizos*
and their descendents [*sic*]; our future is realized in healing that
suffering." Copeland issues the enduring challenge of the cross:

> For lived conversion of heart, mind, and action is not what
> someone else must do, but *who we must become.* So it is in
> our social dis-order, not some other, that racism, sexism,
> economic exploitation, homophobia obtain; it is our con-
> sciousness that is permeated with these disgraces, not some-
> one else's. The cross of Jesus evokes our integrity; calls us
> to responsibility for one another; calls us to entrust our lives
> and futures to the dangerous Jesus.[57]

This is where we may yet become a repentant community that
"lives in memory of the life and ministry, suffering and death and
resurrection of Jesus of Nazareth."[58] Lived conversion through
solidarity and unlearning our racial ignorance through experience of the mirror of blackness forms the crossroads to which we
are called, the place where our hearts may be re-tuned by Jesus,
the place where we may yet find the grace to work through the
contradictions of white male privilege. Do we risk a journey to
these crossroads? Our black Catholic, Latina, Asian, and First
American brothers and sisters call us to these crossroads, in the
fullness of love and forgiveness, where we may yet glimpse the
gift of reconciliation—the illumined wonder of who we are in the
loving embrace of our particularity and communion through Jesus
Christ.

Notes

[1] M. Shawn Copeland, "Theology at the Crossroads: Ebony Word,
Dark Hope" (keynote address at the Uncommon Faithfulness: The
Witness of African American Catholics Conference, University of
Notre Dame, Notre Dame, IN, March 11, 2004).

² M. Shawn Copeland, "Racism and the Vocation of the Christian Theologian," *Spiritus* 2 (2002): 27.

³ I owe a heavy debt to my black Catholic brothers and sisters who addressed the issue of Catholic reception of black theology in the December 2000 issue of *Theological Studies*. I also want to acknowledge the insights I received from responses from Laurie Cassidy and Barbara Hilkert Andolsen to early drafts of this essay.

⁴ Birgit H. Helander, "Nicholas of Cusa as Theoretician of Unity," in *Nicholas of Cusa on Christ and the Church*, ed. Gerald Christianson and Thomas M. Izbicki (New York: Brill, 1996), 314–15.

⁵ Ibid., 315.

⁶ Hugh Lawrence Bond, "Introduction," in *Nicholas of Cusa: Selected Spiritual Writings*, trans. Hugh Lawrence Bond (Mahwah, NJ: Paulist Press, 1997), 43.

⁷ Helander, "Nicholas of Cusa as Theoretician of Unity," 314–15.

⁸ Ibid. See also Nicholas of Cusa, "On Seeking God," in Bond, *Nicholas of Cusa*, 227.

⁹ Bond, "Introduction," 40.

¹⁰ Clyde Lee Miller, *Reading Cusanus: Metaphor and Dialectic in a Conjectural Universe* (Washington, DC: Catholic University of America Press, 2003), 10.

¹¹ Mark Fuhrer, "The Consolation of Contemplation in Nicholas of Cusa's *De Visione Dei*," in Christianson and Izbicki, *Nicholas of Cusa on Christ and the Church*, 239.

¹² Ibid.

¹³ Bond, "Introduction," 39–40; see also Nicholas of Cusa, "Dialogue on the Hidden God," in Bond, *Nicholas of Cusa*, 210–11.

¹⁴ Ibid.; see also Nicholas of Cusa, "On the Vision of God," in Bond, *Nicholas of Cusa*, 253.

¹⁵ Louis Dupré, "The Mystical Theology of Cusanus' *De Visione Dei*," in Christianson and Izbicki, *Nicholas of Cusa on Christ and the Church*, 215. Dupré further explains that "Cusanus has eliminated [a] conception of the mystical life, characteristically modern, that separates that life as an exceptional privilege from a fully continuous religious quest. He has, I think, successfully reversed the trend that severs the highest flowering of the religious mind from its lower intellectual and affective stages, a trend that was to result in modern naturalism. Both theologians and spiritual writers could have greatly profited by his work, if they paid any attention to it" (220).

[16] Louis Dupré, *Passage to Modernity: An Essay in the Hermeneutics of Nature and Culture* (New Haven, CT: Yale University Press, 1993), 187.

[17] Nicholas of Cusa, "On Learned Ignorance," in Bond, *Nicholas of Cusa*, 202.

[18] Bond, "Introduction," 41.

[19] Morimichi Watanabe, "St. Nicholas Hospital at Kues as a Spiritual Legacy of Nicholas of Cusa," in *Nicholas of Cusa and His Age: Intellect and Spirituality*, ed. Thomas Izbicki and Christopher M. Bellitto (Boston: Brill, 2002), 219.

[20] M. Shawn Copeland, "The New Anthropological Subject at the Heart of the Mystical Body of Christ," *Proceedings of the Catholic Theological Society of America* 53 (1998): 25–47.

[21] Ibid.; see also Gustavo Gutiérrez, *On Job: God-talk and the Suffering of the Innocent*, trans. Matthew O'Connell (Maryknoll, NY: Orbis Books, 1987), xiii, cited in Copeland, "Racism and the Vocation of the Christian Theologian," 26.

[22] Copeland, "Racism and the Vocation of the Christian Theologian," 26.

[23] Ibid.

[24] Ibid.

[25] Ibid. Copeland cites John 1:39.

[26] Copeland, "The New Anthropological Subject at the Heart of the Mystical Body of Christ," 42.

[27] Helmut Peukert, *Science, Action, and Fundamental Theology: Toward a Theology of Communicative Action*, trans. James Bohman (Cambridge, MA: MIT Press, 1984), 209, cited in Copeland, "The New Anthropological Subject at the Heart of the Mystical Body of Christ," 42.

[28] M. Shawn Copeland, "Memory, Emancipation, and Hope: Political Theology in the 'Land of the Free,'" *The Santa Clara Lectures* 4, no. 1 (November 9, 1997), 7.

[29] Ibid., 11.

[30] Ibid., 43.

[31] Copeland, "The New Anthropological Subject at the Heart of the Mystical Body of Christ," 31.

[32] Ibid., 33.

[33] Ibid., 33 and 45.

[34] Cynthia Levine-Rasky, ed., *Working through Whiteness: International Perspectives* (Albany: State University of New York Press, 2002), 2.

[35] Margaret E. Guider, "White Privilege and Racism," *Proceedings of the Catholic Theological Society of America* 57 (2002): 132.

[36] My language echoes that of Gustavo Gutiérrez in *We Drink from Our Own Wells: The Spiritual Journey of a People* (Maryknoll, NY: Orbis Books, 1984), 108.

[37] Jamie T. Phelps, "Communion Ecclesiology and Black Liberation Theology," *Theological Studies* 61, no. 4 (December 2000): 695.

[38] Ibid., 11.

[39] Dr. Martin Luther King Jr., "Where Do We Go from Here: Chaos or Community?" in *A Testament of Hope: The Essential Writings of Martin Luther King, Jr.*, ed. James M. Washington (San Francisco: Harper and Row, 1986), 561.

[40] M. Shawn Copeland, "Guest Editorial," *Theological Studies* 61, no. 4 (December 2000): 603–8.

[41] Bernard J. F. Lonergan, *Insight: A Study of Human Understanding* (London: Longmans, 1957), 191–206, 218–44; idem, *Method in Theology* (Minneapolis: Seabury Press, 1979), 231.

[42] See, for example, Laura Pulido, "Rethinking Environmental Racism: White Privilege and Urban Development in Southern California," *Annals of the Association of American Geographers* 90, no. 1 (2000): 6.

[43] Jon Nilson, "Confessions of a White Racist Catholic Theologian" (presidential address), *Proceedings of the Catholic Theological Society of America* 58 (2003), 78–79.

[44] Barbara Andolsen, *Daughters of Jefferson, Daughters of Bootblacks: Racism and American Feminism* (Macon, GA: Mercer University Press, 1986), xiii.

[45] James W. Perkinson, *White Theology: Outing Supremacy in Modernity* (New York: Palgrave MacMillan, 2004), 89.

[46] Ibid., 94.

[47] W. E. B. Du Bois, *The Souls of Black Folk* (1903; reprint New York: Barnes and Noble Classics, 2003), 9.

[48] W. E. B. Du Bois, *Darkwater* (New York: Harcourt Brace and Co.; reprint New York: Schocken Books, 1969), quoted in Perkinson, *White Theology*, 97.

[49] Ibid., 97, 192.

[50] Perkinson, *White Theology*, 117–18.

[51] Ibid., 193.

[52] Ibid., 75.

[53] Copeland, "Racism and the Vocation of the Christian Theologian," 21.

[54] Copeland, "The New Anthropological Subject at the Heart of the Mystical Body of Christ," 41.

[55] Antonio Gramsci, quoted in Ruth Frankenberg, *The Social Construction of Whiteness: White Women, Race Matters* (Minneapolis: University of Minnesota Press, 1993), 240.

[56] Peukert, *Science, Action, and Fundamental Theology*, 206, cited in Copeland, "The New Anthropological Subject at the Heart of the Mystical Body of Christ," 41.

[57] Copeland, "Memory, Emancipation, and Hope," 15.

[58] Ibid., 10.

PART IV

RESOURCES FOR TEACHING AND (UN)LEARNING WHITE PRIVILEGE

QUESTIONS FOR FURTHER REFLECTION AND DISCUSSION

1. Confessions of a White Catholic Racist Theologican

1. Address Jon Nilson's question: How could the marginalization of racism as a theological issue and of black theology as worthy of Catholic theological engagement come to be normal, legitimate, accepted, and utterly unremarkable? How could we Roman Catholic theologians have done this with untroubled consciences?

2. Explore the history of the U.S. Catholic Church's engagement with the legacy of slavery, lynching, Jim Crow, and racism. How should theologians, ethicists, citizens, and people of faith engage this history today? If the legacy of slavery, lynching, and racism endures, how does it endure? How is this history perpetuated?

3. Draw upon Nilson's analysis of the four factors that he argues are chiefly responsible for white Catholic theological racism—the realities of segregation, the ideal of integration, the impact of Vatican II in the United States, and the style of early black theology—to discuss how white Catholic privilege and racism operate.

4. Discuss the basis of Nilson's argument that "there are many good reasons for white Catholic theologians to have marginalized black theology. But these reasons are 'good' in the sense of *explanatory*, not 'good' in the sense of *exculpatory*, not good enough to refute the charge of racism, however nonviolent our racism has been." How would you describe the responsibility that white Catholic theologians bear for privilege and racism?

5. What does Nilson's argument suggest for concrete actions and ways in which white theologians and people of faith can begin to take responsibility for white privilege and racism?

2. White Economic and Erotic Disempowerment

1. Describe your own interpretations of *erotic* and *empowerment*? What does Hobgood mean by *erotic empowerment*? Compare and contrast.

2. How does Hobgood establish her claim that whites project self-hatred onto peoples of color? How do white self-alienation and racism disempower whites and peoples of color?

3. Hobgood invites whites to look into the mirror of blackness. What do white projections of blackness reveal about whites? What should whites do with what we learn about ourselves?

4. What is the problem of "the philosopher's disease"? How does this apply to white theologians?

5. In the context of privilege and oppression described by Hobgood, how should white theologians and people of faith attempt to recover the traditional Christian mandate to integrate self-love and neighbor-love? What does Hobgood suggest? What do you suggest?

3. Social Justice, the Common Good, and New Signs of Racism

1. According to Barbara Andolsen, why should theologians and ethicists draw upon the social sciences and many other disciplines to understand racism?

2. According to Andolsen, how does whiteness as a socially constructed racial category carry advantage?

3. What do Andolsen's research and analysis reveal about the assumptions, attitudes, and practices of white Americans in relationship to race and racism?

4. What are the consequences of black and white Americans interpreting race differently in the aftermath of Hurricane Katrina?

5. What does Andolsen suggest about the way social-science disciplines should be integrated into the practice of theology and ethics?

4. White Privilege

1. What does Charles Curran reveal about the way he engaged and failed to engage white privilege and racism in his theological journey?

2. Curran cites Peggy McIntosh's famous essay "White Privilege: Unpacking the Invisible Knapsack." How does Curran apply McIntosh's work to his autobiography? Read McIntosh's essay and identify the unearned privileges you share with McIntosh. Would you add any privileges to McIntosh's list? Develop a similar review of your unearned disadvantages. Share these lists in groups and discuss: How do unearned privileges and disadvantages relate to each other? What do you notice in the relationship between privileges and disadvantages among members of the group? What do the patterns reveal in relation to society?

3. How may autobiographical reflection inform the critique of white privilege and racism? What might be problematic about white narratives from the perspective of peoples of color?

5. The Dysfunctional Rhetoric of "White Privilege" and the Need for "Racial Solidarity"

1. What does Roger Haight mean by the "dysfunctional rhetoric of 'white privilege'"?

2. What further analyses of the forms whiteness has taken in various U.S. social, political, economic, and historical contexts might foster deeper understanding of the ways whiteness and privilege operate in the United States?

3. Discuss how Haight develops a dialectic between negative contrast experience and racial solidarity.

4. How does Haight appropriate James Cone's *Martin and Malcolm*? How should whites draw upon the legacies of Dr. King and Malcolm X? Are both Dr. King and Malcolm X necessary for whites to address privilege? Why or why not?

6. Moral Imagination and the *Missio ad Gentes*

1. According to Guider, how is racism an obstacle to the vision of *missio ad gentes*?

2. Explain what Guider means when she states that racism "is one of the most serious forms of counter-witness to the gospel"? What historical examples come to mind?

3. In what ways can missionary activity reinscribe white privilege and enact racism?

4. After a confession of racism, what would genuine acts of repentance entail?

5. What would it be like to allow children to be a conscience and guide for us to confront white privilege and racism? How do we dare to take into account the attitudes that are being internalized by privileged children at Catholic schools in the United States and around the world?

7. The Transformative Power of the Periphery

1. What is the "option for the poor," and how does Pfeil view this idea in relationship to white privilege and racism?

2. How does Pfeil describe the "standpoint" of whiteness?

3. What is the "ocular epistemological illusion," and how does it function in relationship to the moral blindness of white people?

4. Explain Pfeil's connection between commodification and egolessness as integral to renouncing the material binds of white dominance?

8. "Becoming Black with God"

1. According to Cassidy, how might Cone's language interrupt the blindness of "whiteness"?

2. Why does Cassidy argue that "becoming Black with God" is necessary for whites to relate authentically to self, others, and God?

3. Why does Cassidy suggest praying to a God who is imagined as black and female? How would or should a white person go about praying to a God who is black and female? Describe images, metaphors, and symbols that you use in prayer. What do they reveal about God and about you? Do the same in relationship to images, metaphors, and symbols used in religious congregations and institutions where you live, work, study, and worship. Do the images privilege any one racial interpretation of the divine?

4. What would it mean for whites to "become Black with God" racially, spiritually, theologically, and morally?

9. (Un)Learning White Male Ignorance

1. What are the three kinds of "learned ignorance" described by Nicholas of Cusa?

2. How does Mikulich relate Cusa's learned ignorance, theologically and morally, to white privilege and racism?

3. What does learned ignorance suggest about lifelong learning?

4. Why does a reinterpretation of learned ignorance (through M. Shawn Copeland) suggest that whites gain insight into the ways peoples of color view whites?

5. Discuss the role of memory for whites to address privilege and racism. What does learned ignorance that draws upon memory and looks into the mirror of "black double-consciousness" suggest about ways whites might develop an alternative moral imagination?

A SELECT THEOLOGICAL
AND SOCIAL-SCIENCE BIBLIOGRAPHY
OF WHITE PRIVILEGE

Bonilla-Silva, Eduardo. *Racism without Racists*. Lanham, MD: Rowman and Littlefield, 2003.

Cone, James. "Theology's Great Sin." *Union Seminary Quarterly Review* 55, nos. 3–4 (2001): 1–15.

Connecticut Roman Catholic Bishops. *Common Ground, Common Good: Toward Greater Social, Economic, and Environmental Justice in Connecticut* (April 1, 2003). Available from http://www.oua-adh.org/CT%20Bishops'%204.1.03%20Eng.htm.

Copeland, M. Shawn. "Guest Editorial." *Theological Studies* 61, no. 4 (December 2000): 603–8.

———. "Racism and the Vocation of the Theologian." *Spiritus: A Journal of Christian Spirituality* 2, no. 1 (Spring 2002): 15–29.

D'Andrea, Michael, and Judy Daniels. "Exploring the Psychology of White Racism through Naturalistic Inquiry." *Journal of Counseling and Development* 77 (Winter 1999): 93–101.

Delgado, Richard, and Jean Stefancic. *Critical Race Theory: The Cutting Edge*. Philadelphia: Temple University Press, 2000.

Frankenberg, Ruth. *White Women, Race Matters: The Social Construction of Whiteness*. Minneapolis: University of Minnesota Press, 1993.

Feagin, Joe. *Systemic Racism: A Theory of Oppression*. New York: Routledge, 2005.

Fine, Michele. *Off White: Readings on Race, Power, and Society*. New York: Routledge, 1997.

George, Cardinal Francis. *Dwell in My Love: A Pastoral Letter on Racism* (2001). Available from http://www.archchicago.org/cardinal/dwellinmylove/dwellinmylove.shtm.

Goldberg, David Theo. *Racist Culture: Philosophy and the Politics of Meaning*. Cambridge: Blackwell, 1993.

Harvey, Jennifer, Karin Case, and Robin Hawley Gorsline, eds. *Disrupting White Supremacy from Within: White People on What We Need to Do*. Cleveland, OH: Pilgrim Press, 2004. (A good resource for undergrad exploration of social location.)

Helms, Janet. *A Race Is a Nice Thing to Have: A Guide to Being a White Person or Understanding the White Person in Your Life*. Topeka, KS: Content Communications, 1992. (Concise text with exercises to help whites understand psychological stages of racial consciousness and identity.)

Hobgood, Mary E. *Dismantling Privilege: An Ethics of Accountability*. Cleveland, OH: Pilgrim Press, 2000. (Very effective undergraduate text.)

Jacobsen, Matthew Frye. *Whiteness of a Different Color: European Immigrants and the Alchemy of Race*. Cambridge, MA: Harvard University Press, 1998.

Johnson, Allan. *Privilege, Power, and Difference*. Mountain View, CA: Mayfield Publishing Company, 2001.

King, Martin Luther, Jr. "Letter from Birmingham City Jail." In *A Testament of Hope: The Essential Writings of Martin Luther King, Jr.*, edited by James M. Washington, 289–302. San Francisco: Harper and Row, 1986.

Levine-Rasky, Cynthia. *Working through Whiteness: International Perspectives*. Albany: State University of New York Press, 2002.

Linebaugh, Peter, and Marcus Rediker. *The Many-Headed Hydra: Sailors, Slaves, Commoners, and the Hidden History of the Revolutionary Atlantic*. Boston: Beacon Press, 2000. (Winner of the International Labor History Award.)

Lipsitz, George. *The Possessive Investment in Whiteness: How White People Profit from Identity Politics*. Philadelphia: Temple University Press, 1998.

Massingale, Bryan N. "James Cone and Recent Episcopal Teaching on Racism." *Theological Studies* 61, no. 4 (December 2000): 700–730. (Outstanding analysis of weaknesses of U.S. Catholic episcopal letters addressing race and failure to address white privilege.)

McIntosh, Peggy. "White Privilege and Male Privilege: A Personal Account of Coming to Understand Correspondences through Work in Women's Studies." Working Paper 189. Wellesley, MA: Wellesley Center for Research on Women, 1988. Available online. (A classic that is invaluable for all educational levels.)

Melczek, Bishop Dale. *Created in God's Image: A Pastoral Letter on the Sin of Racism and a Call to Conversion* (2003). Available from http://www.dcgary.org/bishop/PastoralLetterII.htm.

Mills, Charles. *The Racial Contract*. Ithaca, NY: Cornell University Press, 1997.

Morrison, Toni. *Playing in the Dark: Whiteness and the Literary Imagination*. New York: Random House Vintage Books, 1992.

Myser, Catherine. "Differences from Somewhere: The Normativity of Whiteness in Bioethics in the United States." *American Journal of Bioethics* 3, no. 2 (Spring 2003): 1–11.

Omi, Michael, and Howard Winant. *Racial Formation in the United States: From the 1960s to the 1990s*. 2nd ed. New York: Routledge, 1994.

Perkinson, James W. *White Theology: Outing Supremacy in Modernity*. New York: Palgrave Macmillan, 2004.

———. *Shamanism, Racism, and Hip-Hop Culture*. New York: Palgrave Macmillan, 2005.

Phelps, Jamie. "Communion Ecclesiology and Black Liberation Theology." *Theological Studies* 61, no. 4 (December 2000): 672–99.

Pulido, Laura. "Rethinking Environmental Racism: White Privilege and Urban Development in Southern California." *Annals of the Association of American Geographers* 90, no. 1: 12–40.

Roediger, David. *Working toward Whiteness: How America's Immigrants Became White*. New York: Basic Books, 2005.

Rothenberg, Paula. *White Privilege: Essential Readings on the Other Side of Racism*. New York: Worth Publishers, 2002.

West, Cornel. *Race Matters*. New York: Vintage Books, 1993.

Wildman, Stephanie. *Privilege Revealed*. New York: New York University Press, 1996.

Wijeyesinghe, Charmaine L., and Bailey W. Jackson, eds. *New Perspectives on Racial Identity Development: A Theoretical and Practical Anthology*. New York: New York University Press, 2001.

A SELECTION OF WEB RESOURCES

http://www.uwm.edu/~gjay/Whiteness/
Excellent selection of resources to explore whiteness. Site maintained by Professor Gregory Jay of the University of Wisconsin at Milwaukee.

http://www.nd.edu/~wpconf/
White Privilege: Implications for the Catholic University, the Church, and Theology Conference. All presentations from this conference, held at the University of Notre Dame, Notre Dame, Indiana, March 26–28, 2006, are available for viewing. All presentations are useful for faculty, and the presentations by Peggy McIntosh and Janet Helms are particularly helpful for introducing white privilege to undergraduates.

http://www.osjspm.org/social_teaching_documents.aspx
Catholic social-teaching documents including papal encyclicals and pastoral letters of US Catholic bishops maintained by the Office of Social Justice of the Diocese of St. Paul, Minnesota.

http://www.edchange.org/multicultural/
Outstanding multicultural resources for all educational levels. Maintained by Professor Paul C. Gorski and EdChange.

http://kirwaninstitute.org/
Interdisciplinary research institute for the study of race and ethnicity at Ohio State University founded by John Powell. Powell's post-Katrina analysis of race and poverty in New Orleans and in other regions is available on this site in PowerPoint. Excellent for courses exploring spatial segregation.

http://www.nbccongress.org/
National Black Catholic Congress website includes a variety of biblical, moral, spiritual, social, educational, and political reflection and commentary from the perspective of African American Catholics.

http://www.nypl.org/research/sc/sc.html
New York Public Library Schomburg Center for Research in Black Culture. Includes "Lest We Forget: The Triumph over Slavery," "Digital Schomburg," "Malcolm X: The Search for Truth," and "The Louis Armstrong Jazz Oral History Project," among other resources. The site provides students with information about the legacy of slavery and the wide variety of contributions of African Americans.

http://www.pbs.org/race/000_General/000_00-Home.htm
Online companion to California Newsreels three-part series examining race in society, science, and history. Very helpful introductory site for undergraduates.

http://www.pbs.org/independentlens/strangefruit/
Explores the story behind the haunting lyrics of Billie Holiday's "Strange Fruit," the protest song of the 1940s that influenced the civil rights movement and endures today. The site also provides a helpful exploration of protest music over the past century.

http://www.tolerance.org/
Outstanding resources for social change for teens, parents, and teachers from the Southern Poverty Law Center. Students find the "Tolerance Watch," "Do Something," and "Dig Deeper" areas especially helpful.

CURRENT PRACTICES

A Selection of Catholic Dioceses and Institutions Integrating Anti-Racist Vision Statements and Action Plans

Archdiocese of Chicago

Inspired by Cardinal Francis George's pastoral letter *Dwell in My Love*, the Archdiocese of Chicago is in the midst of a twenty-year plan to eradicate racism in the archdiocese and society. The website provides information about the history, strategy, faith context, and Chicago's Anti-Racism Team responsible for implementing the long-term plan at http://www.dwellinmylove.org/. In addition to developing short- and long-term goals and program evaluation, the Anti-Racism Team facilitates a variety of workshops for parishes and other institutions in the diocese.

Diocese of Gary, Indiana

Bishop Dale J. Melczek's pastoral letter *Created in God's Image* includes an anti-racism initiative: http://www.dcgary.org/bishop/CreatedInGodsImage.pdf.

Pax Christi USA

Pax Christi USA initiated a twenty-year plan to transform the national peace organization into an anti-racist, multicultural movement for peace with justice. Pax Christi believes that this transformation can only be achieved by developing "organizational structures that foster mutual respect and dialogue and which create accountability to people of color; policies which affirm the dignity and talents of every person; practices which hold multiple and at times conflicting perspectives in creative tension; and decision-making processes which depend on and incorporate the multi-cultural

identity that is the Church, the Body of Christ." http://www
.paxchristiusa.org/pc_brothers_sisters_more.asp?id=695.

NETWORK, A Catholic Social Justice Lobby

The board and staff of this nationally recognized Catholic social
justice lobby initiated a self-review of institutional racism in 2002.
NETWORK provides resources for citizens and people of faith to
reflect and act to dismantle white privilege and racism. In addition
to links to Catholic pastoral letters addressing racism and suggested
actions to develop anti-racist public policies, these resources include:

- The Leaven Center: Offers "Doing Our Own Work: A Seminar
  for Anti-Racist White Women." http://www.leaven.org/
  doow.htm.
- Crossroads Ministry: Works to build anti-racist multicultural
  institutions primarily by facilitating workshops that train institutional anti-racism teams guided by principles of peace with
  justice. For example, Crossroads facilitated the development of
  Pax Christi's Anti-Racism Team. See its links to other anti-racism resources and religious institutions that have utilized training by Crossroads. http://www.crossroadsministry.org/.

Institute for Recovery from Racisms

The Institute for Recovery from Racisms, founded and directed
by Reverend Clarence Williams, CPPS, trains individuals and institutions in an alternative approach that focuses on "racial sobriety."
The institute is made up of more than two hundred certified facilitators in twenty states and in three countries. The institute offers workshops, trains facilitators, and designs programs for various educational, civic, religious, and corporate organizations. http://
www.racialsobriety.org/index.htm.

CONTRIBUTORS

Barbara Hilkert Andolsen is Helen Bennett McMurray Associate Professor of Social Ethics at Monmouth University, West Long Branch, New Jersey. In addition to numerous articles addressing social ethics, she is author of *Daughters of Jefferson, Daughters of Bootblacks: Racism and American Feminism* (Mercer University Press, 1986) and *The New Job Contract: Economic Justice in an Age of Insecurity* (Pilgrim Press, 1999).

Laurie M. Cassidy is Assistant Professor of Religious Studies at Marywood University, Scranton, Pennsylvania. Her most recent publication, "Affirming *Imago Dei*: Implications of the Black Catholic Congress Movement's Reception of *Rerum Novarum* no. 32 for Moral Reasoning in Suffering," appeared in the *Journal of Catholic Social Thought* 3 (Winter 2006): 39-55. She received a master of arts in Christian spirituality from Creighton University, a master of theological studies from Weston Jesuit School of Theology, and a Ph.D. in theological ethics from Loyola University Chicago. She was drawn to the study of theological ethics through anti-racist work with inner-city youth in Boston.

Charles E. Curran is Elizabeth Scurlock University Professor of Human Values at Southern Methodist University. His latest book is *Loyal Dissent: Memoir of a Catholic Theologian* (Georgetown University Press, 2006).

Margaret E. Guider, O.S.F., is Associate Professor of Missiology and Chair of the Pastoral Studies Department at the Weston Jesuit School of Theology, Cambridge, Massachusetts. Her publications include *Daughters of Rahab: Prostitution and the Church of Liberation in Brazil* (Augsburg Fortress, 1995) and *What Child Is This? Children in Christian History and Theology* (Augsburg Fortress, forthcoming).

Roger Haight is Visiting Professor of Systematic Theology at Union Theological Seminary, New York. His latest book is *The Future of Christology* (Continuum, 2005). Haight is a member of the Society of Jesus (Jesuits) and is a past president of the Catholic Theological Society of America.

Mary Elizabeth Hobgood is Associate Professor of Religious Studies at College of the Holy Cross, Worcester, Massachusetts. She teaches Christian social ethics with a specialization in economic and feminist ethics. Her publications include *Catholic Social Teaching and Economic Theory* (Temple University Press, 1991) and *Dismantling Privilege: An Ethics of Accountability* (Pilgrim Press, 2000).

Alex Mikulich is Assistant Professor of Religious Studies and Theology at Saint Joseph College, West Hartford, Connecticut. He earned a master of divinity degree from the Weston Jesuit School of Theology and a Ph.D. in theological ethics from Loyola University, Chicago. His "Mapping 'Whiteness': The Complexity of Racial Formation and the Subversive Moral Imagination of the 'Motley Crowd'" appeared in the *Journal of the Society of Christian Ethics* 25, no. 1 (Spring/Summer 2005): 99-122. In the early 1990s he was educated into the struggle against racial and class segregation by homeless people in the Tenderloin District of San Francisco.

Jon Nilson is Associate Professor of Systematic Theology at Loyola University Chicago. He is the author of *Nothing beyond the Necessary: Roman Catholicism and the Ecumenical Future,* as well as numerous articles in both popular periodicals and professional journals. He is a member of the Jewish-Catholic Scholars Dialogue in Chicago, the Anglican-Roman Catholic Consultation in the United States, and serves on the editorial board of *Theological Studies.* He is a past president of the Catholic Theological Society of America.

Margaret R. Pfeil is Assistant Professor of Theology at the University of Notre Dame. She earned an M.T.S. from the Weston Jesuit School of Theology and a Ph.D. from the University of Notre Dame. She is a founder and resident of St. Peter Claver Catholic Worker House in South Bend. Her articles have appeared in *Louvain Studies, Josephinum Journal of Theology, The Journal for Peace and Justice Studies*, and the *Mennonite Quarterly Review*.